STANDARD GAUGE GREAT WESTERN 4-4-0s
PART 2
COUNTIES TO THE CLOSE 1904—1961

T0145465

No 3715 *City of Hereford*: an 'official', in photographic
grey, in the plain green era. *(British Railways)*

STANDARD GAUGE
GREAT WESTERN 4-4-0s
PART 2
COUNTIES TO THE CLOSE
1904–1961

O. S. NOCK

BSc, CEng, FICE, FIMechE

No 3434 *Joseph Shaw. (British Railways)*

DAVID & CHARLES

NEWTON ABBOT   LONDON

NORTH POMFRET (VT)

British Library Cataloguing in Publication Data

Nock, Oswald Stevens
   Standard gauge Great Western 4-4-0s
   Part 2: 'Counties' to the close, 1904-1961
   1. Locomotives—England—History   2. Great Western
   Railway (Great Britain)
   I. Title
   385'.36'10942   TJ603.4.G72G7

ISBN: 978-1-4463-0647-5

Library of Congress Catalog Card Number 78-62486

© O. S. NOCK 1978

All rights reserved. No part of this publication may be
reproduced, stored in a retrieval system, or transmitted, in
any form or by any means, electronic, mechanical, photo-
copying, recording or otherwise, without the prior
   permission of David & Charles (Publishers) Limited

Set and printed in Great Britain
by Biddles of Guildford
for David & Charles (Publishers) Limited
Brunel House Newton Abbot Devon

Published in the United States of America
by David & Charles Inc
North Pomfret Vermont 05053 USA

CONTENTS

Down West of England express passing Southall, hauled by an unidentified County class 4-4-0.
(H. Gordon Tidey)

PREFACE

In taking up the second stage in the history of this fascinating group of locomotives, the age in which they all in some way became subject to the Churchward standardisation, it is natural that the outside-cylinder Counties are cast for a major role. These are certainly one of those locomotive classes around which a wealth of misconceptions have arisen—or been created and fostered by those who think they know it all. They have been written down as one of Churchward's 'failures', in the same way that the stature of *The Great Bear* has been whittled down by some scribes. In this book I have tried to show how in the first place they were a direct result of Churchward's keen and penetrating interest in American locomotive practice, and secondly to show what excellent locomotives they were on the road. There is no doubt that they were rough riders, but so were many other famous types of which I have had plenty of experience on the footplate! The Counties filled a very important niche in the general pattern of Great Western motive power.

Then, this book is concerned with the general process of standardisation applied to the large group of outside-framed 4-4-0s in the provision of standard boilers with superheaters and top feed apparatus, as rapidly as possible after 1910. It is evident however that the fitting of piston valves in place of the original slide valves was not considered so important. A number of the Bulldogs and Flowers still retained slide valves to the time of their eventual withdrawal. The majority of these locomotives were subject to

Up local train leaving Twyford, hauled by No 3309 *Maristow. (H. Gordon Tidey)*

several boiler changes during their lengthy lifetime. These were largely the result of interchangeability of the different types of boiler during the transition period from parallel to the long-cone taper variety, and those readers anxious to study such details can be referred to the publications of the Railway Correspondence & Travel Society. The more interesting changes from the 2-row to the single-row Swindon superheater, which came eventually to affect most locomotives fitted with the No 2 boiler, are not recorded chronologically for each locomotive.

In the preparation of this book I am once again much indebted to many friends in and out of the railway service: to Kenneth J. Cook, who succeeded to part of the chief mechanical engineer's responsibilities on the Western Region, when the department was fragmented after the retirement of F. W. Hawksworth; to the late H. Holcroft, and his lifelong interest in Great Western locomotive affairs, and to the running superintendents and locomotive inspectors who provided me with footplate experience. To the late E. L. Bell I am particularly indebted, because he was not only a keen and experienced recorder of train running, but in his later years spent much of his time collecting and tabulating all that he found, from any source, published about British locomotive working. I was the fortunate recipient of these voluminous notes after his death. Then I am also indebted to Messrs J. C. Keyte and the late A. V. Goodyear, who both made such a close study of locomotive running on the main lines north and south of Birmingham. As I emphasised in prefacing the first volume of this work, I always view locomotive history with an eye to the end product, that is the capacity of a locomotive as a revenue earner. Our knowledge of the standard gauge 4-4-0s of the GWR would be the poorer in this respect but for the careful work of men like Bell, Goodyear and Keyte.

O. S. NOCK

Silver Cedars,
High Bannerdown,
Batheaston,
Bath.   *February 1978*

CHAPTER ONE

AMERICAN INFLUENCE

In studying the second phase of development of the standard gauge 4-4-0s of the Great Western Railway, steps must be retraced to the turn of the century. It had then been generally agreed among those members of the board directly concerned that sooner or later Churchward would succeed Dean as Locomotive, Carriage and Wagon Superintendent—as the office was then titled. In confidential discussions Churchward had been authorised to begin developing his own ideas on locomotive and carriage design. The first tangible outcome was the famous drawing of 1901, illustrating his proposed new standard classes for working the entire main line traffic of the railway. This drawing included an express passenger 4-4-0. With the benefit of hindsight several modern writers have questioned the wisdom of this inclusion, and stigmatised the County class that eventuated as the least successful of all Churchward's standard classes; but Churchward did not design and build locomotives without very cogent preliminary investigation, and to appreciate what was in his mind the situation in the late 1890s must be reviewed.

Although the policy of passenger traffic development was being pursued with great vigour after the final abolition of the broad gauge, the need for very large new locomotives was at first small. These would obviously need much careful experimenting and scrutiny when they were first put into traffic, and while the train services themselves were being developed the 4-4-0 locomotives, first of the Badminton series, and then the Atbaras were proving more than adequate for all current requirements. Nor

indeed was there any likelihood of the 4-4-0 being outdated for some time to come. While the 10-wheelers, whether of the Atlantic or of the 4-6-0 type, were intended for the long non-stop runs with trains that were expected to become progressively heavier, there was a diversity of other services, that did not require such large locomotives. Furthermore, there were engineering restrictions on certain important routes that in the early 1900s precluded the use of 4-6-0s. That in some cases these restrictions were based on quite empirical considerations rather than fundamental scientific reasoning is beside the point at this stage in the present book.

When K. J. Cook read his paper on the Churchward locomotive development to the Institution of Locomotive Engineers in March 1950, Sir William Stanier in the subsequent discussion made a breezy reference to the introduction of the County class, saying that it was designed particularly with the west-to-north route from Bristol to Shrewsbury in mind. At that time, over the joint line north of Hereford, the LNWR was responsible for the track maintenance, and would not then consider the use of large 4-6-0 locomotives. But the service was a very important one, and had some heavy trains. As Sir William Stanier put it, 'Churchward was not going to be told by Old Webb what he could do', so he built the biggest 4-4-0 that would be accepted—a far more powerful locomotive than anything the LNWR was using over that same route at the time. I was present at that meeting, and in company with several of my colleagues thought that Stanier had been a little 'off the beam' in referring to

Churchward's rival on the West to North route: F. W. Webb's Jubilee class 4-cylinder compound *La France*, normally LNWR No 1926 but temporarily renumbered as the 4000th locomotive built at Crewe. *(British Railways)*

Webb, because at the time the Counties were actually introduced, in 1904, Webb had been retired more than a year. It must be remembered of course that the basic idea of the County was shown on the drawing of 1901 when Webb was still very much a power in the land! Any stipulations from Crewe, however, were likely to have reached Churchward indirectly, because Webb had by 1901 become very much aloof from fraternising with his contemporaries, particularly as at that time Churchward was still nominally in a subordinate position.

After much study of the situation it does seem that the origin of the County class was almost entirely due to American influence. It has frequently been said that Churchward seemed instantly to know a good thing when he saw it, and the centrepiece of his standard 2-cylinder design was wholly American. In W. F. Pettigrew's classic work *A Manual of Locomotive Engineering*, published in 1899, A. F. Ravénshear of the Patent Office contributed a section on American and continental locomotives, and in respect of the former he wrote:

The cylinders are sometimes cast separately and secured to a distance piece between the frames, forming a saddle on which the smokebox rests. But the plan most generally followed is to employ two castings only, each casting forming one cylinder and half the saddle. The two castings are bolted together at the centre of the engine. The result is a much more rigid connection than where there are three castings, and at the same time several steam-tight joints are avoided.

The accompanying drawing is reproduced from Pettigrew's book, and shows a design incorporating slide valves, with the port face marked B. The faces marked D and E are those of the steam and exhaust passages, while in this design, as necessitated by the use of slide valves the steam chest, G, is a separate box. An important feature that was to become a salient point in future Great Western designs is the recess F, which contained the frame bar. Quite apart from the cylinder construction and the framing however, the 4-4-0 type as developed in the USA was so much the universal type of main line, or 'road' locomotive as to become generally known as the 'American'. Alfred W. Bruce has written:

The 4-4-0 type was one of the simplest and most accessible engines ever built. It was well balanced for riding stability as it had an ideal three-point frame support in the centre-pin of the leading four-wheel truck and the two driving-wheel-equalizer fulcrums. For many years the bolsters of the leading trucks were rigid, and often the front driving tyres were made flangeless to suit sharp curvature. Because of their balance and riding stability they were well adapted to high speeds under adverse track conditions.

The main rods were always coupled to the front drivers, thereby providing space for and accessibility to, the Stephenson inside valve gear which was generally used on these engines. No other type of engine was so well adapted to the use of this valve gear. The driving springs were often underhung, an arrangement that provided easy riding, but at the same time permitted the engine to 'roll' laterally on its springs at high speeds. Although cases of overturning have been known, they were extremely rare.

The 4-4-0 type was retired too soon to receive generally piston valve cylinders, outside valve gear, and superheat, but it was one of the most attractive types ever built because of its simplicity and well-balanced

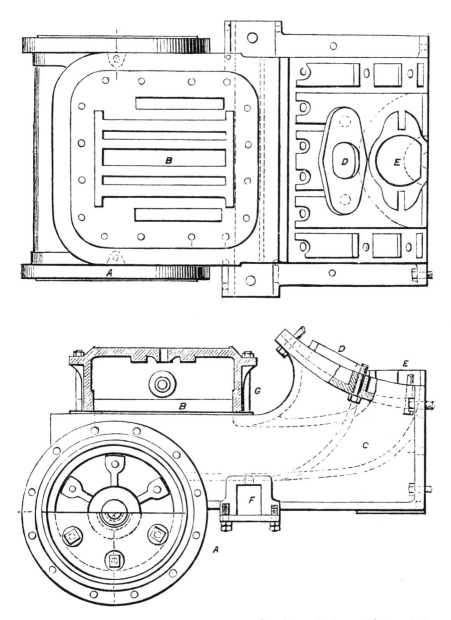

American cylinder and half smokebox saddle.

proportions. The first ones were built with a deep, short, and narrow firebox that was dropped down between the driving axles and also between the frames, leaving only enough space above the rail for the ashpan. As more and more grate area was required for larger engines, the bottom of the firebox was raised, first above the rear driving axle and then above the frames.

The above was written in 1952, in a scholarly and comprehensive valediction to the steam locomotive in America, and Bruce concludes this particular reference:

On the whole the 4-4-0 type was very flexible in both design and operation, light and easily handled. Over 25,000 of these engines were built in the United States from 1840 to 1905, although very few were built between 1900 and 1905.

A typical 'American' type: the Chicago & North Western 'Fast Mail' 4-4-0. *(Author's collection)*

New York Central 4-4-0 No 999, used on the Empire State Express. *(Author's collection)*

Second of Churchward's County class, No 3474 *County of Berks*, after fitting with cast-iron chimney. *(P. J. T. Reed)*

There can be little doubt that with a continuing need for 4-4-0 locomotives on the GWR Churchward felt that there was a greater field for development with the American style of design than with the traditional British inside-cylinder version, and the County is explained as a logical class to be included in the scheme of standardisation propounded in the drawing of 1901. So far as the wheelbase was concerned, the County bore a remarkable resemblance to two of the best known American 4-4-0s of the 1890s, the Chicago & North Western Fast Mail class, and the legendary 999 of the New York Central. The fixed wheelbase was 8ft 6in on all three classes, while the total engine wheelbase was 24ft 8in (CNW), 23ft 11in (NYC) and 24ft 0in (GWR). The coupled wheel diameters were 7ft 2in, 6ft 8in and 6ft 8½in respectively. If to this similarity one adds the frame and bogie design, and the tapered boiler barrel and 'wagon-top' firebox, as the Americans called it, the County is seen as a very faithful Anglicised version of the 'American' type.

None of these features was exclusive to the Counties in the new standard range of Great Western locomotives. They were in fact common to them all. It was in the proportioning of the wheelbase that the Counties stood alone. The inside-cylindered Cities had the same fixed wheelbase, but they had the Dean outside-framed bogie, with wheel centres at 6ft 6in, in complete contrast to the bar-framed type on the County, which was pure American. As first used on Churchward's standard locomotives it had a rectangular frame of flat bar to which four pairs of pedestals were attached at their upper end and which were braced below by diagonal and horizontal ties. The pairs of pedestals served for horn blocks to carry the axleboxes. The frame carried no weight but merely held the bogie axles in position, as this was done by equalisers spanning the axleboxes on each side. The

equalisers were in pairs with a laminated spring between them and the buckle of this butted under the frame. Above the frame at this point a pair of transverse beams on the top of the frame and midway between the wheels carried between them the upper ends of swing links which allowed lateral movement of the bogie. The bogie centre pin was embraced by a centre bearing in the form of a casting provided with legs to carry the lower ends of the links. The wheelbase was 7ft 0in and the wheel diameter 3ft 2in.

In another respect, however, the Counties differed from long-established American practice, and indeed from Churchward's Atlantics and 4-6-0s. In quoting Bruce, earlier reference is included to the 3-point suspension of the locomotive, by the use of compensating beams between the axleboxes of the coupled wheels. While Churchward used a form of compensation on his 4-6-0s, the coupled wheels of the Counties were independently sprung; thereby hangs something of a tale, to be told when I come to the performance of the Counties in traffic. So far as the frames were concerned, while adopting American practice in principle, the main sections carrying the coupled wheel anxlebox guides were of plate, instead of bar construction. By 1900 the art of welding had progressed in America to a point at which it had been possible to produce commercially a one-piece welded frame, though usually the front section, or rail as it was called, was made separately to facilitate repair in case of damage. No welding was however used on the frames of the Counties. At the front end each side consisted of a thick rectangular slab attached to the buffer beam at the front end. The back end had to be splayed out to a reduced thickness to suit the depth of the main frame plate, and a joint between the

Churchward's standard cylinder and valve chest.

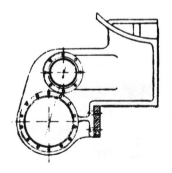
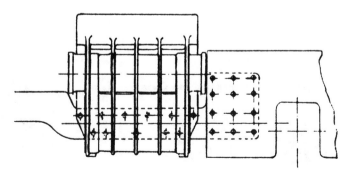

front and main frames was made immediately behind the cylinders. This arrangement is shown in the accompanying drawing.

The cross-sectional view shows the very neat design of cylinder and valve chest. It is important to emphasise how this back-to-back arrangement, bolted together on the centre line of the locomotive as in American practice, formed the centrepiece of the standardisation programme. The cylinder blocks were the same on both sides, and standard for all the classes having 18in × 30in cylinders, and 10in diameter piston valves. The pattern for the cylinders carried alternative saddles for the boilers, one to suit the smokeboxes of boilers No 1 and No 4, and the other for Nos 2 and 3. The latter differed in diameter of smokebox and in vertical distance between the centre lines of cylinders and boiler. The centre line of the cylinders in all the standard types was by Churchward's insistence always horizontal. By the time that the Counties were built the new standard arrangement of the Stephenson link motion had been determined, with a maximum travel of 6¼in and a *negative* lead of 0.15in in full gear. This gave a hearty 'punch' when starting away, or when the lever was well forward for climbing a heavy gradient. A comparison between the motion details of the City and County classes is interesting, thus:

Locomotive class	city	county
Valves	Slide	10in piston
Maximum travel	4⅜ in	6¼ in
Steam lap	1⅛ in	1⅝ in
Exhaust clearance	NIL	NIL
Lead in full forward gear	³⁄₁₆ in	−0.15in
Cut-off in full gear	74%	77½%

Both classes had the No 4 standard boiler, but by reason of the larger cylinders the County had

No 3478 *County of Devon* at Laira shed, with original type copper-capped chimney and experimental lettering on tender. *(P. J. T. Reed)*

a nominal tractive effort of 20,530lb at 85 per cent working pressure, against 17,790lb. No doubt it was expected that the improved valve gear of the Counties would result in a more economical use of the steam, and that the same boiler would be adequate.

The first of the new locomotives, No 3473 *County of Middlesex* was completed at Swindon in May 1904, and it is interesting to recall contemporary comment. *The Locomotive* had an official broadside view as early as its issue of June 1904, and drew attention to the I-section connecting rods, solid-bushed big-ends, and that all the locomotive wheels were braked. The general effect was distinctly angular, with the vertical step in the running-plate immediately ahead of the cylinders, and the rather gaunt 'ladder' up which the crew had to climb from rail level to the footplate. The chimney externally was parallel rather than of the tapered type used on the Atbaras and Cities, and handsomely finished with a copper cap. There was a pleasing lithographed colour plate of the *County of Middlesex* in the July 1905 issue of *The Railway Magazine*. In that journal Charles Rous-Marten made one of his strangest pronouncements. In November 1904 he wrote:

It has long been an open secret that Mr Churchward contemplated following the example set by Mr Ivatt, Mr Aspinall, Mr Robinson, and Mr Worsdell, and building an engine of the Atlantic type. It might indeed be said that in one sense he has done this already, having imported one Atlantic from France. But it was understood that he intended to construct one at Swindon which should be virtually an *Albion* without her trailing pair of coupled wheels, and with a small pair of carrying wheels behind the firebox. Before doing so, however, he preferred to experiment with the County class, which are in most points identical with the City type, but, like

Albion have 30-inch piston stroke, which necessitated the use of outside instead of inside cylinders.

Furthermore, in the 100th number of *The Railway Magazine*, October 1905, in a general survey of locomotive practice he repeated the assertion that the Counties '. . . were mainly on the lines of the City type, and in many respects absolutely identical . . .' From what I have already written in this opening chapter, I think it could be agreed that there were never two classes built so quickly after each other from the same works that were *less* alike!

The first ten Counties, built between May and October 1904 were named and numbered as tabulated, the numbers following a batch of 30 Bulldogs Nos 3443-3472 that came after the completion of the Cities:

No 3475 *County of Wilts* in original condition. *(Real Photographs)*

Number	Name
3473	*County of Middlesex*
3474	*County of Berks*
3475	*County of Wilts*
3476	*County of Dorset*
3477	*County of Somerset*
3478	*County of Devon*
3479	*County of Warwick*
3480	*County of Stafford*
3481	*County of Glamorgan*
3482	*County of Pembroke*

The first was finished in the old style, with red-brown underframes and the entwined letters GWR on the centre panel of the tender, but some experiments were in progress with the tender lettering, and some of this first batch had the letters GWR in block characters, one on each of the lined-out panels, while others had all three letters closely grouped on the centre panel.

The second batch of 20 locomotives, turned out with great rapidity in October to December 1906, was numbered from 3801 to 3820. These had tapered cast-iron chimneys like the City class, and the full name *GREAT WESTERN* on their tenders, together with the gartered crest. They also had black underframes, with orange lining. The first ten were named after Irish counties, in support of the vigorous efforts then being made by the traffic department to develop the tourist business via Fishguard and Rosslare. It is evident from the rapid multiplication of the class up to 30 units within two years that there was general satisfaction with them. The class was actually the most numerous of all the new 'standards' at the end of 1906, the comparable numbers of other classes being 19 4-6-0s, 13 4-4-2s, and 20 2-8-0s. The Atlantic total given does not include the French compounds.

For a period of about 18 months, between November 1907 and May 1909, No 3805 *County Kerry* carried a standard No 2 boiler. To keep the boiler centre-line the same as on the others of the class, a special distance piece was inserted between the saddle and the smokebox. At the same time an experimental plate-frame bogie that had previously been used on standard

Atlantic No 184 was substituted for the American bar-framed type.

In service the Counties acquired a reputation for rough riding, again in contrast to the smooth action of the Cities. In his book *Swindon Steam 1921-1951* K. J. Cook writes:

> They tended to develop considerable hammering in the left-hand trailing axleboxes, caused by the amount of counterbalance to the reciprocating parts of the motion which had to be concentrated in the four wheels. The short rigid wheelbase was also a factor.

The effect of locomotives on the track, and upon their own riding had been studied by some locomotive engineers, notably by my old teacher, Professor W. E. Dalby, at Imperial College. It was not until after World War I that the civil and mechanical engineers of the British railways really got together on the subject, and the searching analysis of the Bridge Stress Committee produced some surprising results. In view of the embargo placed upon the use of 4-6-0 locomotives over certain routes, it is amusing to study the effects of hammer-blow produced by various standard types of Great Western locomotive.

The accompanying table sets out the values of hammer-blow, or dynamic augment to the dead weight on the axles at a speed of 6 revolutions per second. This represents a speed of 86mph in the case of locomotives with coupled wheels 6ft 8½in diameter, and 73mph in the case of a Bulldog. It will be noticed that in the outside-cylinder classes the wheel hammer-blow is nearly as great as the whole axle, thus providing an explanation of Cook's remarks about hammering on one side. It will also be seen that so far as maximum, combined effect was concerned the County was the worst of the lot. A

Saint would have had less damaging effect on the track. Even after the findings of the Bridge Stress Committee had been made public there were still lingerings of old ideas among civil engineers. On the Bristol-Birmingham route that included the use of running powers over the Midland line between Yate and Standish Junction, the governing factor so far as locomotive usage was concerned was a viaduct at Stonehouse. When eventually the LMS lifted the restriction it was only to permit the use of 2-cylinder 4-6-0s, which it will be seen from the table had a considerably worse effect on the track than the 4-cylinder Stars!

Heavy-footed as they were upon the track the Counties were by no means the worst among the locomotives examined by the Bridge Stress Committee. A superheated Dunalastair IV 4-4-0 of the Caledonian had a maximum combined axle load of 31 tons; this was surpassed by a figure of 33.2 tons from a South Eastern & Chatham L class 4-4-0, and the zenith was reached by a North Eastern R class 4-4-0 with a murderous 36.2 tons. As to confrontation with the LNWR on the Shrewsbury-Hereford Joint Line, the Bridge Stress Committee did not quote any figures for Webb 4-cylinder compounds, which were working some of the through expresses when the Counties were first introduced, but the George the Fifth class 4-4-0s hit up a healthy 33.2 tons. At the same time a devastating combined axle load did not necessarily mean rough riding. The SECR L class, and the NER R class are among the smoothest steam locomotives on which I have ever travelled, whatever they might have been doing to the track.

Before leaving the matter of balancing, attention must be drawn to the figures relating

BALANCING OF GWR LOCOMOTIVES

Type	Class	Speed at 6rps (mph)	Maximum static axle (tons)	Hammer-blow (tons)			Max. combined load at 6 rps (tons)	
				Whole locomotive	Axle	Wheel	Axle	Wheel
4-4-0	Flower	86	18.0	12.9	6.5	3.6	24.5	12.6
4-4-0	City	86	18.5	12.9	6.5	3.6	25.0	12.8
4-4-0	Bulldog	73	17.6	12.9	6.5	3.6	24.1	12.4
4-4-0	County	86	19.4	16.6	8.5	8.0	27.9	17.7
4-4-2T	2221	86	19.0	16.6	8.5	8.0	27.5	17.5
4-6-0	Saint	86	18.4	17.9	6.9	6.4	25.3	15.6
4-6-0	Star	86	19.7	13.7	2.9	1.9	21.5	11.2
4-6-0	King	84	22.5	12.2	4.0	2.6	26.5	13.8

No 3818 *County of Radnor* in photographic grey, showing the standard Churchward style of lining-out. *(British Railways)*

to the so-called County Tanks, or more correctly the 2221 class. These were sometimes referred to as a tank engine version of the County class, and so far as wheels, cylinders and motion went they certainly were, but they carried the No 2 boiler instead of the No 4. It seems that Churchward wanted to use the No 4, but that the weight came out too heavy, and there was a proposal in 1905 to introduce a 4-4-4 tank, with a larger coal bunker and the No 4 boiler. As can be seen from the table on page 16 the 2221 had a heavy enough axle loading, despite use of the No 2 boiler, and one can well appreciate that the experiment in October 1906 of building one of them, No 2230, with a No 4 boiler did not last long. Twenty of the 2221 class were built non-superheated in 1905-9, and a further ten superheated in 1912.

The introduction of brakes on the bogie wheels on the Counties was an example of the very close attention given to braking on the GWR from the original decision of the company to adopt the vacuum rather than the Westinghouse air brake in 1880 and to develop and manufacture its own equipment. Use of 25in of vacuum, instead of the 20-22in on other railways, provided an excellent brake maintained by the distinctive crosshead pump, rather than an ejector, though there were sometimes buffing shocks when operating trains of mixed stock, as on the West-to-North route on which a certain amount of LNWR coaching stock was in regular use. Very often however, on many railways, one

would find that the locomotive was the most lightly-braked unit in the whole of a passenger train, and Churchward sought to remedy this, first by applying a high degree of brake power to the coupled wheels, and then to brake the bogie wheels as well. This latter involved problems with flexible connections, and needed careful maintenance. It had been Great Western practice to use steam brakes on the locomotives, working with vacuum brakes on the trains; on the Counties, in common with all Churchward's standard locomotives, vacuum braking was used throughout. However, after Churchward had retired, brakes on the bogie wheels were discarded as being not worth the trouble in fitting and maintaining them.

The Counties had the sparse shelter and simple layout of the Churchward standard cab. The first 30 of the class, built using saturated steam, had lever reverse, and on the right-hand side they could be distinguished from the final ten, which were superheated when new in 1911-12, by having the reversing rod horizontal and passing in front of the splashers. This was made all the more prominent on the earlier locomotives of the class by being highly polished as shown in the picture of *County of Devon* on page 14. Those with screw reverse had the rod inclined downwards from the cab, passing behind the leading coupled wheel splasher. The photographic section of the locomotive department at Swindon was highly skilled at 'doctoring' official photographs to represent individual locomotives, but this practice had its pitfalls. A photographer named Gothard, at Barnsley of all places, produced a postcard montage of the Reading accident of June 1914, of which I saw the immediate aftermath, and this included a portrait of the *County of Leicester*, which was hauling the up Worcester express. This locomotive, one of the 1906 batch, had by then been superheated, but the portrait included in the montage was not only doctored from an 'official' included in a postcard series issued by the GWR and actually showing No 3818 *County of Radnor*, but was turned inside-out, to suit the layout of the montage. Not only was the locomotive shown in its original non-superheated condition with tapered cast-iron chimney, but also with the left-hand side masquerading as the right, and consequently minus the reversing rod!

To complete the story of the locomotives originally built non-superheated, before passing on to their early performance, I must add that Nos 3811 to 3820 were named after English and Welsh counties, though one might question the inclusion of Leicestershire, which did not lie within the Great Western orbit. Other more obvious titles, such as Oxford, Gloucester and Cornwall, were still omitted. In days before World War I, however, the through Newcastle-Bournemouth expresses were worked by Great Western locomotives from Oxford shed throughout between Leicester and Basingstoke, whereas in the period between the two world wars Great Central, or LNER locomotives worked southwards to Oxford. At the time of the Reading accident *County of Leicester* was in charge of an Oxford driver, and could well have been one of those taking turns to Leicester, via the Banbury-Culworth Junction link and the Great Central main line. Another of that same batch, No 3814, was originally misnamed *County of Cheshire*. This was corrected to *County of Chester* after about six months. The names of the 3801-3820 series were:

No	Name	No	Name
3801	*County Carlow*	3811	*County of Bucks*
3802	*County Clare*	3812	*County of Cardigan*
3803	*County Cork*	3813	*County of Carmarthen*
3804	*County Dublin*	3814	*County of Chester*
3805	*County Kerry*	3815	*County of Hants*
3806	*County Kildare*	3816	*County of Leicester*
3807	*County Kilkenny*	3817	*County of Monmouth*
3808	*County Limerick*	3818	*County of Radnor*
3809	*County Wexford*	3819	*County of Salop*
3810	*County Wicklow*	3820	*County of Worcester*

CHAPTER TWO

EARLY PERFORMANCE OF THE *COUNTIES*

In December 1904 No 3473 *County of Middlesex* was put through some tests with the dynamometer car. Some years ago at Swindon I had the privilege of studying the rolls of these tests, and quite apart from the speeds run and the power developed, they showed some most interesting characteristics. I must add that at the time of their recording the results were not subjected to the close scrutiny that became customary in later years. I was fortunate enough to enjoy the friendship of that most expert and objective of locomotive testing engineers, S. O. Ell, and quite apart from making the original rolls available to me, with many a shrewd comment, he had many stories to tell of earlier years at Swindon. He told me how after a test had been made Churchward would have the roll spread out in the drawing office, but make no more than the most cursory examination. He had a marvellous way of quickly assessing the merit or otherwise of performance, putting his rule over the record here and there to measure speed and drawbar pull. Then, if the cut-off was right and the drawbar pull adequate that was all that mattered.

Strange as it may seem today, no one bothered about coal consumption. If the boiler performance and output from the cylinders was good in relation to the cut-off, it was taken for granted that the fuel consumption was economical.

It was the performance of the de Glehn compound *La France* that seemed to set the parameters for Churchward's development, and with the arrangement of the Stephenson's link motion skilfully worked out at Swindon, it was possible to obtain an equally good performance out of the 4-6-0 locomotive *Albion* working in about 17 to 18 per cent cut-off, with regulator fully open. At the time the *County of Middlesex* was tested, in December 1904, doubts had evidently arisen as to whether this was the best way to work the new locomotives. In my own footplate experience on a number of the Churchward 2-cylinder classes, Saints, and those derived from them such as Halls, Granges and the Hawksworth Counties, I found that if

One of the Irish batch: No 3808 *County Limerick* in running colours. *(British Railways)*

19

pulled up inside about 22 per cent they developed a kicking action, which would no doubt be transmitted back to the leading coaches of the train. Be that as it may, in the dynamometer car tests of No 3473 in 1904, at times the cut-off was 18 per cent with full regulator, and at others 25 per cent with a partial opening—all in running between Paddington and Swindon on level, or easily graded track.

The second of the dynamometer car test runs, made on 21 December 1904 gave the more significant results, because the load was the relatively heavy one for that period on the GWR, of 260 tons on 44 axles. There were several checks in the early stages, and steady running was not obtained until some distance after Reading. Then the roll showed a very much smoother pull at 25 per cent, with a narrow regulator opening than at 15 per cent. Comparative details of the working were:

Location	Speed mph	Cut-off %	Regulator opening	Drawbar pull - tons
Goring	60 ½	25	¼	1.6
Moreton Cutting	62	15	¾	1.3

The boiler pressure remained constant throughout at a little below 200lb. per sq in.

Between Didcot and Swindon continuous use of 18 per cent cut-off gave a speed of 58½ to 61½mph on this gradually rising length, with a drawbar pull at 58½mph on 1 in 754 of 1.75 tons, equal to 1.9 tons on level track. The equivalent drawbar horsepower was 665. One of the best performances of *Albion* on the same stretch of line, when being worked somewhat harder, gave 1100 equivalent drawbar horsepower. Although the difference in tractive effort between the 4-6-0 and 4-4-0 locomotive was due only to the higher boiler pressure, *Albion* had a grate area nearly 30 per cent larger.

The test train of 21 December 1904 stopped at Swindon, and then continued to make an interesting start-to-stop run to Bath, as shown in detail in the accompanying table. Seeing that a cut-off of 42 per cent was used initially, the immediate start from Swindon was not very rapid, but it will be seen that the regulator was opened wider as cut-off was reduced. Cut-off was then continuously at 18 per cent until the train was checked by signal in the approach to Bathampton. The performance may not appear to be anything very wonderful with a load of no more than 260 tons, but Great Western coaching stock of the Dean era had a notoriously high rolling resistance. No very precise inferences, however, may be drawn from these

DYNAMOMETER CAR TEST RUN — 21 DECEMBER 1904
Load: 11 vehicles, 260 tons
Locomotive: No 3473 *County of Middlesex*

Distance Miles		Actual min sec	Speed mph	Regulator opening	Cut-off %	DP pull tons
0.0	SWINDON	0 00	—	—	—	—
0.7	*Milepost 78*	2 25	—	¼	42	2.2
1.7	*Milepost 79*	4 06	41 ½	½	42	2.65
2.7	*Milepost 80*	5 24	49	¾	18	1.7
5.6	Wootton Bassett	8 33	61	¾	18	1.5
7.95	*Milepost 85 ¼*	10 44	66	¾	18	1.45
8.2	*Milepost 85 ½*	—	—	shut	—	—
9.2	*Milepost 86 ½*	—	70 ½	¼	18	—
10.4	Dauntsey	12 54	71	¼	18	0.4
10.95	*Milepost 88 ¼*	—	69	½	18	1.25
13.7	*Milepost 91*	15 42	71	½	18	1.25
16.7	Chippenham	18 30	63	½	18	—
18.7	*Milepost 96*	20 25	61 ½	full	18	1.45
21.0	Corsham	22 45	61	full	18	1.45
—	*Milepost 98 ¾*	—	—	¼	18	—
—	*Milepost 99 ¾ **	—	66	shut	—	—
—	*Milepost 100 ¾ **	—	67 ½	¼	18	—
24.6	Box	26 08	70	¼	18	—
—	*Milepost 103 ¼*	—	—	—	—	—
		sigs.	30 ½	—	—	—
26.7	*Milepost 104*	28 50	—	¾	25	2.5
27.3	Bathampton	29 48	42	¾	25	2.35
28.4	*Milepost 105 ¾*	31 12	50 ½	shut	57	—
29.6	BATH	33 45	—	—	—	—

* Mileposts in Box Tunnel

test results; while the sustained 61mph up the 1 in 660 gradient from Chippenham to Corsham involving an actual drawbar pull of 1.45 tons indicated a resistance of 9.2lb/ton, which is not much greater than that of modern BR stock, the pull of 1.75 tons on the 1 in 754 gradient between Wantage Road and Challow suggested a resistance of about 12lb/ton. It will be seen from the table that the engine ran freely at 66-67mph with the regulator shut on both the short 1 in 100 descents. It would have been interesting to see test results from a County worked hard from Wellington up to Whiteball Tunnel, as I described with *City of Bristol*, in the first volume of this work.

One of Rous-Marten's earliest runs with the Counties was made from Bristol to Exeter. Although Churchward was evidently prepared to make alterations in the regular engine working for him, and to ensure the best possible results

Up Cheltenham express at Swindon, hauled by No 3474 *County of Berks*. *(British Railways)*

by the provision of a locomotive inspector on the footplate, he never granted a footplate pass. No details are available therefore of the actual technique of driving employed. The run with No 3479 *County of Warwick* is set out alongside a contemporary one on the same train with a very heavily-loaded Atbara class 4-4-0. The schedule for the non-stop run of 75.6 miles was 85 minutes. There was an important difference in the weather conditions on the two occasions, for while the Atbara had a calm day, and was able to average 63.5mph over the 36.6 miles from Nailsea to Taunton with its 335-ton train, the County had to contend with such a furious side wind off the Severn estuary as to take nearly six

North to West express passing Patchway, with GWR and LNWR stock, hauled by No 3815 *County of Hants*. *(L & GRP)*

4-4-0 *Atbara*, after having been renumbered 4120, and fitted with superheater and top feed. *(Author's collection)*

minutes longer for the same distance, despite the best efforts of Driver Burden—who made the record run with *City of Bath* in July 1903—and Inspector Greenaway. When they came to more sheltered conditions south-west of Taunton, the County made much better time up to Whiteball. The minimum speed recorded was 30.2mph, against 20.4mph by the Atbara. Rous-

Marten recorded that the lowest speed of the *County of Warwick* on the 1 in 80 approaching the tunnel was 30.2mph, and that this was sustained on the 1 in 127 through the tunnel to the summit. This suggests an equivalent drawbar horsepower of about 700.

Details of another interesting run were taken by Rous-Marten on the 12.07pm up from Exeter non-stop to Paddington, with a substantial load of 305 tons. The principal interest of this run lies

GWR BRISTOL-EXETER

Run No:		1		2	
Locomotive No:		3479		3388	
Locomotive Name:		*County of Warwick*		*Sir Redvers*	
Load, tons		295		335	
Distance Miles		Actual min sec	Average speeds mph	Actual min sec	Average speeds mph
0.0	BRISTOL	0 00	—	0 00	—
6.0	Flax Bourton	9 20	38.6	9 50	36.6
8.1	Nailsea	11 28	59.0	11 58	59.0
12.0	Yatton	15 05	64.7	15 27	67.2
15.6	Puxton	18 32	62.6	18 41	66.7
16.8	*Worle Junc*	19 43	60.8	19 25	60.8
20.3	Bleadon	23 08	61.4	23 02	66.3
24.2	Brent Knoll	27 25	54.6	27 00	59.1
27.0	Highbridge	30 39	51.8	29 28	67.8
30.8	Dunball	35 24	48.0	33 10	61.7
33.3	BRIDGWATER	38 28	49.2	35 33	62.8
39.1	Durston	45 31	49.3	41 03	63.2
44.8	TAUNTON	51 54	53.6	46 38	61.2
46.8	Norton Fitzwarren	54 07	52.6	48 51	54.2
51.9	Wellington	60 08	50.8	54 37	53.1
55.7	*Whiteball box*	66 15	37.3	62 54	27.5
60.7	Tiverton Junc	71 17	59.6	68 29	53.7
63.0	Cullompton	73 21	66.8	70 37	64.7
67.2	Hele	77 06	67.2	74 13	70.0
68.4	Silverton	78 07	70.8	75 18	66.6
72.1	Stoke Canon	81 27	66.6	78 40	66.0
75.6	EXETER	85 10	—	82 08	—

GWR 12.07pm EXETER-PADDINGTON
Load: 305 tons, full
Locomotive: No 3474 *County of Berks*

Distance Miles		Actual min/sec	Average speeds mph
0.0	EXETER	0 00	—
3.5	Stoke Canon	5 40	37.1
7.2	Silverton	9 49	53.5
8.4	Hele	11 11	52.8
12.6	Cullompton	15 43	55.7
14.9	Tiverton Junc	18 28	50.2
19.9	*Whiteball Box*	24 58	46.2
23.7	Wellington	28 54	57.5
28.8	Norton Fitzwarren	33 05	73.1
30.8	TAUNTON	34 42	74.3
36.5	Durston	39 43	68.4
42.3	BRIDGWATER	45 27	60.6
—		pws	—
48.6	Highbridge	52 46	43.5
58.8	*Worle Junc*	62 31	63.1
63.6	Yatton	67 46	66.3
69.6	Flax Bourton	73 18	65.0
74.5	Bedminster	77 34	68.9
74.9	*Pylle Hill Junc*	78 46	19'0
76.6	*Bristol East Junc*	82 02	31.5
86.7	BATH	93 46	51.6
99.6	CHIPPENHAM	109 43	48.4
105.9	Dauntsey	115 42	63.0
110.7	Wootton Bassett	121 17	51.5
116.3	SWINDON	127 26	54.8
122.0	Shrivenham	132 57	62.0
127.1	Uffington	137 32	66.7
133.2	Wantage Road	143 02	66.5
137.1	Steventon	146 29	67.8
—		sigs.	—
140.5	DIDCOT	151 17	42.5
148.8	Goring	160 03	51.4
152.1	Pangbourne	163 03	66.0
157.6	READING	168 02	66.0
162.6	Twyford	172 34	66.0
—		sigs slight	—
169.4	Maidenhead	179 09	61.9
171.1	Taplow	181 02	54.2
175.1	SLOUGH	184 47	64.0
180.4	West Drayton	189 43	64.4
—		sigs slight	—
184.5	Southall	194 15	54.7
187.9	Ealing Broadway	197 46	58.2
193.6	PADDINGTON	204 22	—

Net time 197 minutes

in its vigorous start from Exeter up to Whiteball, and the fast run down the Wellington bank, which took the train through Taunton in the good time of 34 minutes 42 seconds from the start. The speed at Whiteball summit was 38½mph, but in an account of the run in *The Engineer* Rous-Marten states that the locomotive was eased up the final 1 in 115 gradient past Burlescombe; I think it was more likely that there was some drop in boiler pressure after the hard work on the earlier part of the ascent from Exeter. Whatever may have developed approaching Whiteball, however, they put on a tremendous spurt after Norton Fitzwarren, when the gradients had flattened out to little easier than level, particularly in the average of 74.5mph from Taunton to Durston. The permanent way check near Bridgwater was a bad one, but speed was finely recovered, and by passing Bedminster, 74.5 miles, in 77 minutes 34

seconds—74 minutes net—an extremely fine performance had been put up, with a load of 305 tons. Onwards over the generally level extent of the rest of the journey to London, signal checks at Didcot, Maidenhead and Southall, together with the long slowing over the Bristol avoiding line, did not prevent the 162.8 miles from Taunton to Paddington being covered in 169 minutes 40 seconds, excellent sustained work for a 4-4-0 with a load of 305 tons. The average speeds from station to station are set out in the accompanying log, but I should add that the minimum speed at Whiteball summit was 38½mph, and on Dauntsey bank 47½mph. This run is also interesting as showing how the Counties were used on the crack West of England trains while there were still no more

Oxford-Wolverhampton express on Lapworth troughs, hauled by No 3819 *County of Salop. (H. Gordon Tidey)*

than a few of the larger locomotives in service.

Another interesting run over the 'Bristol & Exeter' was logged by Mr A. V. Goodyear, with No 3479 *County of Warwick*. There was a permanent way restriction past Cowley Bridge Junction that made the immediate start slower than that of *County of Berks* on the 12.07pm up non-stop; the 12.7 miles from Silverton up to Whiteball summit took only 13 minutes 40 seconds, an average of 55.8mph. Speed rose to as much as 66mph at Cullompton, and the minimum speed over the summit was 41mph. What promised to be a fast descent to Taunton was spoiled by a second permanent way check, but some good speed was maintained on the level stretches after Taunton, and the booked time of 86 minutes from Exeter to Bristol was more than kept, despite a signal stop outside Temple Meads, just at the finish.

GWR EXETER-BRISTOL
Load: 228 tons tare, 245 tons full
Locomotive: No 3479 *County of Warwick*

Distance Miles		Actual min sec	Average speeds mph
0.0	EXETER	0 00	–
—		pws	–
3.5	Stoke Canon	6 45	–
7.2	Silverton	10 50	54.3
8.4	Hele	12 07	56.0
12.6	Cullompton	16 05	63.5
14.9	Tiverton Junc	18 37	54.5
18.9	*Milepost 175*	23 06	53.6
19.9	*Whiteball Box*	24 30	42.9
23.7	Wellington	28 04	64.0
—		pws	–
28.8	Norton Fitzwarren	32 54	37.3
30.8	TAUNTON	35 15	51.1
35.8	Cogload Junc	40 08	61.7
42.3	BRIDGWATER	46 10	64.6
48.6	Highbridge	52 04	64.1
51.4	Brent Knoll	54 45	62.6
54.4	Bleadon	58 33	63.2
63.6	Yatton	66 21	63.1
69.6	Flax Bourton	72 49	55.7
74.5	Bedminster	78 09	55.2
—		sig stop	–
75.6	BRISTOL	83 45	–

On a day in April 1905 No 3474 *County of Berks* had the 10.45am Exeter 'non-stop' from Paddington, with a load of 12 coaches, all of the clerestory type and weighing 314 tons gross behind the tender. The following details, taken from the guard's journal, give passing times to no nearer than half-minutes, but a good general impression of the work can be gained from a study of these. The train passed Reading in 41 minutes, but was then subjected to two engineering slacks, one at Goring nominally to

15mph for track repairs, and the second through Swindon station where the subway was being reconstructed. Apparently the driver took a rather liberal view of the first, and was reported for 'skimping' by his guard! Despite this, Swindon was passed slowly in 83½ minutes from Paddington, and with times of 100 minutes through Chippenham, and 112 minutes to Bath, they were round the Bristol avoiding line and over Pylle Hill Junction, 118.7 miles, in 125 minutes. Good work followed, having regard to the long sustained effort required from this 4-4-0 with a heavy train. The 44.1 miles to Taunton were covered in 46 minutes, including recovery from the slow running round the Bristol avoiding line, and then the 10.9 miles up to Whiteball summit were climbed in 14 minutes. The total time over the 173.7 miles from Paddington was 185 minutes and there was plenty of time in hand to cover the slowing for a bridge repair at Stoke Canon and to reach Exeter, 193.6 miles, three minutes early, in 207 minutes.

Two runs from Reading to Paddington logged by Mr Goodyear are indicative of the smart work done by the County class engines on level track with moderate loads. On the first of the two *County Cork* got away briskly from Reading, and was doing 60mph only 3½ miles from the start. After that the 27 miles between mileposts 33 and 6 took 24 minutes 28 seconds, an average of 66.2mph, with a maximum of 70½mph near Slough. With a train heavier by one coach, No 3475 *County of Wilts* was slower off the mark, but worked up to 70mph near Slough, and made a smart start-to-stop average of 56.9mph to the stop at Ealing Broadway. Mr Goodyear also logged a run on which County Tank No 2226 had to tackle a 10-coach corridor dining car train up from Reading. The schedule was a slow one allowing 47 minutes, but the 28.6 miles to passing Hanwell took 32½ minutes, with a maximum speed of 66mph and after a slight signal check an easy run brought the train into Paddington in 42¼ minutes. This run was made on one of the Weymouth trains, which then changed locomotives at Reading.

East of Swindon R. E. Charlewood recorded a very good run on the 12.15pm from Plymouth with No 3481 *County of Glamorgan*, and an exceptional load for that period of thirteen 8-wheelers totalling about 400 tons gross behind the tender. Shrivenham, 5.8 miles, was passed in 9 minutes 26 seconds, and the ensuing 35.5

GWR READING-PADDINGTON

Run No:		1		2	
Locomotive No:		3803		3475	
Locomotive Name:		*County Cork*		*County of Wilts*	
Load (tons)		175		215	
Distance		*Actual*	*Average speeds*	*Actual*	*Average speeds*
Miles		*min sec*	*mph*	*min sec*	*mph*
0.0	READING	0 00	–	0 00	–
5.0	Twyford	7 00	–	7 40	–
11.8	Maidenhead	13 11	65.9	14 10	62.7
13.5	Taplow	14 43	66.5	15 52	60.0
17.5	SLOUGH	18 10	69.5	19 35	64.5
19.8	Langley	20 11	68.7	21 31	70.7
22.8	West Drayton	22 52	67.1	24 22	63.1
26.9	Southall	26 35	66.3	28 11	64.5
29.5	West Ealing	–	–	30 38	63.6
30.3	Ealing Broadway	29 41	65.8	31 55	
34.7	Westbourne Park	33 41	66.0		
36.0	PADDINGTON	36 21	–		

miles to Reading took 33 minutes 56 seconds. Checks followed, first in Sonning Cutting and then at Hayes, but despite this the 71.6 miles to the stop at Ealing Broadway were completed in 77 minutes 20 seconds. The two checks were estimated to have cost 3 minutes between them, leaving a net time of 74¼ minutes and a net average speed of 57.9mph.

Although it has been stated by men who were close to the centre of affairs at Swindon that the Counties were designed for the West to North route via the Severn Tunnel, few of them seem to have been allocated to those duties in early days. The first instance I have been able to trace is a log in one of the notebooks of the Revd W. A. Dunn, on the 9.45am up from Chester in August 1909, when that train was worked by No 3814 *County of Chester* between Shrewsbury and Bristol. Over this section the train, of typically mixed formation, was made up thus: one GWR 6-wheeler, one LNWR eight, one LNWR six, six GWR eights, one LNWR eight, and two GWR eights—12 vehicles in all with a tare weight of 300 tons. The recorder took a detailed note of the ascent from Shrewsbury to Church Stretton, with the times at every milepost, and for a 'cold' start the climbing was extremely good. Speed rose to 31mph on the initial 1 in 127 to milepost 2½, increased to 48mph on the easy pitch

Up West of England express near Acton hauled by No 3807 *County Kilkenny. (Locomotive Publishing Co.)*

between Condover and Dorrington, and then fell to a sustained 28mph on the 1 in 100 past Leebotwood. Milepost 13, adjacent to Church Stretton station, was passed in the good time of 23 minutes 41 seconds from the start. A maximum of 75mph was attained before Craven Arms, and no difficulty would have been experienced in keeping the 63 minutes timing for the 51 miles from Shrewsbury to Hereford; however, adverse signals checked the approach to Leominster, and by the frequency of the checks that followed it was evident that a slower train was just ahead. Eventually the arrival in Hereford was in just 70 minutes from Shrewsbury. The train was then booked non-stop over the ensuing 67.2 miles to Bristol in 101 minutes, not an easy average over a section so complicated by speed restrictions and sharp intermediate gradients. The Revd W. H. Dunn unfortunately gives little detail of what seems to have been a fine performance. The only intermediate timing was at Pontypool Road, to

which the time of 46 minutes 10 seconds for 33.5 miles showed regaining of nearly three minutes of the late start from Hereford. Checks came thick and fast afterwards, including a permanent way check in the depths of the Severn Tunnel, and the total time to Bristol became 104 minutes.

I may add that some good work had evidently been done north of Shrewsbury, where the tare load was 242 tons, hauled by one of the Atbaras rebuilt with City boiler, but in 1909 still non-superheated, No 3406 *Melbourne*. The Revd W. A. Dunn gives only summary times, as follows:

Distance Miles	Schedule minutes	Actual min. sec.
0.0 Chester	0	0 00
12.1 Wrexham	20	19 21
4.8 Ruabon	10	8 44
7.4 Gobowen	13	10 25
18.0 Shrewsbury	21	21 10

West to North express descending the bank from Church Stretton to Shrewsbury, hauled by an unidentified County class 4-4-0. *(British Railways)*

City class 4-4-0 No 3402 *Halifax*, still with original number, but with superheater and top feed apparatus. *(H. W. Burman)*

The first section included the severe Gresford bank, with nearly 4 miles at 1 in 82; up this *Melbourne* went at a really excellent 26mph. The two subsequent stretches are both more adverse than favourable, and it is only after leaving Gobowen that the tendency of this sharply-undulating road turns in favour of the locomotive. Some fast work was necessary to run those concluding 18 miles to Shrewsbury in the scheduled 21 minutes.

In the early 1900s the Paddington-Worcester non-stops leaving at 1.40pm and 4.45pm were prestige trains, though not timed very fast. The former was allowed 135 minutes for the 120.5 miles, while the latter, generally with a much lighter load, 130 minutes. The 1.40pm detached a slip portion at Kingham, and there the hard work of the journey more-or-less ended. The long rise from Oxford certainly continued to Moreton-in-Marsh, seven miles farther on, but so liberal was the point-to-point time from Kingham to Evesham, including the racing descent of the Honeybourne bank—22 miles in 25½ minutes—that time could be readily made up if there was any lateness in passing Kingham. Most of Mr Goodyear's runs on these trains were made with inside-cylinder 4-4-0s, or singles, in all cases working through to Wolverhampton via Worcester, but among his records is an interesting run with No 3804 *County Dublin* on a day when the load out of Paddington was 375 tons.

Seeing that there was a severe engineering speed restriction to come, right down to 10mph over a bridge near Oxford, the start was most leisurely, taking 14¾ minutes to pass Southall, 9.1 miles. One could not attribute this to the heavy load, when on a contemporary run with the same train and the same load one of the Cities took nearly a minute less for this opening length. *County Dublin* then averaged just 60mph from Southall to Reading, passing there 2¾ minutes late in 41 minutes 48 seconds from Paddington, and after the bridge repair slowing was five minutes late through Oxford, 74 minutes 4 seconds for 63.4 miles. Now at last the driver seemed to wake up to the fact that he was somewhat behind time, because a very determined recovery effort began. At the same time long experience in the observance of locomotive performance, both on and off the footplate has led me to hesitate before criticising a run purely on the basis of times taken from a seat in the train. So many factors can affect the working of steam locomotives, of which the ordinary passenger cannot be aware.

The long rise to the summit near Milepost 92 begins just after Wolvercot Junction, at Milepost 67. The actual gradients change constantly, but the average gradient is about 1 in 500. Up this *County Dublin* covered the 10 miles between

Mileposts 70 and 80 in 11 minutes 25 seconds at an average of 52½mph while after the detaching of the slip portion the final 7.1 miles from Kingham to Moreton-in-Marsh took 7 minutes 55 seconds. The lateness had been reduced to four minutes at Kingham, but without exceeding 65½mph down the Honeybourne bank, where *Builth Castle* in 1939 touched 100mph. Evesham, 106.6 miles, was passed in 120 minutes 8 seconds and the last 13.8 miles into Worcester, Shrub Hill, took only 14 minutes 42 seconds to finish the run on time in 134 minutes 50 seconds from Paddington. The load from Kingham had been 285 tons.

The same locomotive made a much better run, albeit with a considerably lighter load, on the 11.25am express from Paddington to Birkenhead in the last months when the principal expresses to Birmingham and the North were running via Oxford. This particular train ran non-stop from Paddington to Birmingham, detaching a slip coach at Leamington, and it was in this latter that the recorder travelled. Details of this run and a faster one with the pioneer locomotive are tabulated herewith. *County of Dublin* started well, passing Southall in 12¼ minutes and attaining 68mph before Slough, but the permanent way check near Maidenhead was a bad one and caused the time through Reading to

be 40¾ minutes, and to Oxford 67 minutes 20 seconds. Good work followed, up the long rising gradients between Oxford and Aynho, where the inclination averages 1 in 650, and where the average speed was 58.4mph. Although passing Fenny Compton in the good time of 100 minutes 10 seconds there was not quite enough in hand to offset the second permanent way check, and the arrival of the slip coach at Leamington was 1½ minutes late.

On the second run *County of Middlesex* had a somewhat delayed start, and for some reason the recorder took no details between Slough and Goring, where the average speed was only 45½mph. Some excellent running was made from Oxford onwards, with an average speed of 63mph to Aynho, and 58.3mph uphill from Banbury to Fenny Compton, though of course even such running as this could not compensate for the earlier delays and the arrival of the slip coach in Leamington was 6¾ minutes behind time. The late R. E. Charlewood gave brief details of a much faster, and practically undelayed run on the same train in the journal of The Railway Club. The engine was No 3479 *County of Warwick*, with a load of 200 tons. Slough was passed in 20 minutes 33 seconds, and speed averaged 67mph on to Reading, which was passed in 36 minutes 8 seconds. Then came a bad signal check at Tilehurst, despite

GWR PADDINGTON-LEAMINGTON (via OXFORD)

Distance Miles		3473 County of Middlesex 220		3804 County Dublin 230	
		Actual min sec	Average speeds mph	Actual min sec	Average speeds mph
0.0	PADDINGTON	0 00		0 00	
5.7	Ealing Broadway	8 50	—	8 55	—
—		pws	—	—	—
9.1	Southall	13 40	42.1	12 15	60.6
18.5	SLOUGH	24 00	55.5	21 10	63.4
—		—	—	pws	—
24.2	Maidenhead	sigs	—	28 35	—
31.0	Twyford	—	—	36 00	55.0
36.0	READING	sigs	—	40 45	63.2
44.8	Goring	48 25	—	49 00	64.0
52.8	*Didcot East Junc*	56 25	60.0	57 05	59.5
—		pws	—	—	—
58.3	Radley	62 25	47.1	62 40	59.0
63.4	OXFORD	67 30	60.2	67 20	64.3
75.1	Heyford	78 55	61.5	79 45	56.5
80.2	Aynho	83 40	64.5	84 55	59.3
86.1	BANBURY	89 05	65.5	90 45	60.8
94.8	Fenny Compton	98 00	58.6	100 10	55.5
—		—	—	pws	—
99.8	Southam Road	102 35	65.4	106 40	—
—		sigs.	—	—	—
105.9	LEAMINGTON	109 40	—	114 35	—

A post-1925 picture of No 3816 *County of Leicester* attached to the 8-wheeled tender from 4-6-2 No 111 *The Great Bear. (L & GRP)*

which Didcot East Junction, 52.8 miles, was passed in 53 minutes 5 seconds. A clear road was obtained until the approach to Leamington, and with Oxford passed in the good time of 63 minutes 24 seconds there was no need for hurry afterwards. There were moderate permanent way checks at Culham and Aynho, and Banbury was passed in 86 minutes 26 seconds; with a maximum speed of 75½mph down the Southam Road bank milepost 103 was passed in 101 minutes 48 seconds. The final approach to Leamington was very slow, as on account of single-line working it was necessary to stop to detach the slip coach. The actual arrival was in 109 minutes 9 seconds from Paddington.

A very interesting run was logged by Mr A. V. Goodyear on the 1.40pm up two-hour Bristol non-stop express with a comparatively heavy load of 295 tons for the year 1907. There was nothing in hand on this run, though from what Mr Goodyear told me on sending his log, I inferred that the driver was not pressing the locomotive unduly, and claimed on arrival at Paddington that none of the time lost was due to the locomotive. He was, as will be noted, a clear three minutes down at Reading, and without checks it would have needed some very hard running for a County to cover the last 36 miles in 33½ minutes to the stop in Paddington. Mr Goodyear estimated the net time as 122½

GWR BRISTOL-PADDINGTON (in 1907)
Load: 278 tons tare, 295 tons full
Locomotive: No 3802 *County Clare*

Distance Miles		Schedule minutes	Actual min sec	Average speeds mph
0.0	BRISTOL (TEMPLE MEADS)	0	0 00	—
1.7	Stapleton Road		4 35	—
4.8	Filton Junc	9	10 46	29.3
7.7	Winterbourne		14 33	46.0
13.0	Chipping Sodbury		20 50	50.6
17.6	Badminton	23½	26 22	50.0
23.4	Hullavington		31 58	62.1
27.9	Little Somerford		35 44	71.6
34.7	Wootton Bassett		42 23	61.4
40.3	SWINDON	43	48 18	56.8
46.0	Shrivenham		53 48	62.2
51.1	Uffington		58 24	66.5
57.2	Wantage Road		64 00	65.5
64.5	DIDCOT	66½	70 25	68.3
69.1	Cholsey		74 50	62.5
76.0	Pangbourne		81 07	65.8
—			sigs	—
81.6	READING	83½	86 30	61.3
86.6	Twyford		92 26	50.6
93.4	Maidenhead		99 00	62.2
—			sigs slight	—
99.1	SLOUGH	100	104 38	60.7
—			sigs.	—
108.5	Southall		114 33	57.5
111.9	Ealing Broadway		119 00	45.8
116.4	Westbourne Park		124 00	54.1
117.6	PADDINGTON	120	126 20	—

Net time 122½ minutes

minutes. Sustained speed up the 1 in 300 from Stoke Gifford to Badminton was exactly 50mph followed by a maximum of 75mph at Little Somerford. On the splendidly favourable stretch from Shrivenham to Didcot speed was held at no more than 66-67mph and this fell away to no faster average than 63.8mph onwards to Tilehurst.

So far as the accelerated trains on which the 4-6-0 locomotives were to distinguish themselves, there are two very interesting records of No 3820 *County of Worcester* on the up Limited, after the opening of the new route via Castle Cary. Both unfortunately are rather lacking in detail. The first was logged by Charles Rous-Marten, and he was clearly very disappointed that the booked 4-6-0, No 2908 *Lady of Quality*, which had worked the train up from Plymouth, ran hot, and had to come off at Exeter. No 3820 *County of Worcester*, then no more than six months out of shops, was commandeered at a moment's notice. Although the load was no more than 190 tons, the ensuing run must have been extremely good, and one could have wished for more detail. The climb to Whiteball was good, but there was a bad delay at Taunton and the train did not really get going again until beyond Cogload, after which it was excellent work to cover the ensuing 42.3 miles on to

CORNISH RIVIERA EXPRESS – IN 1907
Locomotive No 3820 *County of Worcester*

Run No:		1	2
Load, tons full		190	290
Distance *Miles*		*Actual min sec*	*Actual min sec*
0.0	Exeter	0 00	0 00
19.9	*Whiteball Box*	23 46	23 45
30.8	Taunton	34 46	33 45
35.8	*Cogload Junc*	39 01	38 00
58.4	Castle Cary	61 24	61 25
78.1	Westbury	81 50	84 40
173.7	Paddington	177 20	180 10

Westbury, with their adverse gradients and intervening slacks in 41 minutes 49 seconds. It would have been comparatively easy work to cover the remaining 95.6 miles to Paddington in 95½ minutes.

On the second of these two runs No 3820 worked through from Plymouth to Paddington, bringing a load of 200 tons into Exeter, which was increased there to 290 tons. The two runs are tabulated alongside. To Whiteball the two tied to within a second, though the first had the disadvantage of starting 'cold' from Exeter. On

the second run fast running was made down Wellington bank, and Cogload was passed in the good time of 38 minutes from Exeter. After that the heavier load of the second run began to take its toll, and the 42.3 miles from Cogload to Westbury took 46 minutes 40 seconds—no mean performance for all that. From Westbury to Paddington once again the two runs tied exactly, with the second reaching Paddington only 10 seconds outside the three-hour schedule. Seeing that the locomotive had worked through from Plymouth, this was a fine achievement.

Before leaving what could be termed the first decade of Churchward it must be recorded that contemporary opinion, despite the brilliant feats of a few individual locomotives, was far from generally favourable. Particularly among those who set store upon points of lineament and decoration, Churchward was regarded as the man who had done more to spoil the look of British locomotives than anyone then living. Had they lived to see it those critics would no doubt have been astonished beyond all measure at the virtual adoration today of the locomotive dynasty which he founded! With the benefit of hindsight it is easy now to appreciate how this has come about. The grouping of 1923 left Great Western locomotive practice untouched, and in subsequent years the products of Swindon, unsullied with the cross-breeding that came to affect those of Darlington, Doncaster, Eastleigh, and above all those of Crewe, remained entirely traditional to the eye, regardless of the more subtle and significant improvements in constructional practice embarked upon at Swindon. The British railway enthusiast loves tradition, and the once-stigmatised 'ugly' locomotives of Churchward and his successors became top favourites, to the surprise and annoyance of enthusiasts whose partisanship led them elsewhere.

Nor were the critics of Churchward's design style confined to non-professional 'railwayacs', as the enthusiasts of the day were generally known at that time. In the discussion at the Institution of Mechanical Engineers following Churchward's classic paper 'Large Locomotive Boilers', in 1906, James Stirling said that he thought the new Great Western engines were 'not bonnie', and criticised their somewhat angular appearance. There is no doubt that Churchward took this criticism to heart, and on future batches of the standard two-cylinder classes, including the Saints and the Counties,

Up Birmingham express passing Fenny Compton with No 3711 *City of Birmingham.* *(Leslie J. Thompson)*

care was taken to smooth out some of the gaunter features of their appearance, such as the square step-down of the running plate ahead of the cylinders, and the elimination of the 'climbing frame' that gave access to the cab from rail level. These after all were little more than minutiae; the basic appearance remained, on no class more starkly utilitarian than on the Counties.

CHAPTER THREE

FINISHING TOUCHES IN DESIGN

The year 1909 was a milestone in the development of Great Western locomotive practice. Until then the railways of Great Britain generally had been some of the most backward in the adoption of superheating. When J. F. Gairns wrote his classic work *Locomotive Compounding and Superheating*, information in his possession showed that in 1906 out of 287 locomotives fitted with the Schmidt superheater only one was British, the GWR 2-cylinder 4-6-0 No 2901 *Lady Superior*. It has however been claimed equally that the first British adoption of this equipment was on an 0-6-0 goods locomotive of the Lancashire & Yorkshire Railway, by George Hughes. The tardiness of British locomotive engineers in taking up superheating was undoubtedly due to the abundance of good steam coal in this country, and the relatively short runs, which it was thought gave little time for a superheated locomotive really to warm up to its work. Churchward was, of course, ready enough to try any device that gave promise of a reduced coal consumption, though reluctant to adopt in its entirety a proprietary design, and particularly one that had certain strings attached to it, like the Schmidt superheater. In view of the remarkably swift change to superheating that began at Swindon in 1909, and affected the series of locomotives covered in this monograph as much, if not more so, than the large 4-6-0 passenger locomotives, the steps leading to the finalisation of superheater design at Swindon may be recalled, even though they were mentioned in outline in the monograph dealing with the Stars, Castles and Kings.

There were two things about the Schmidt superheater that Churchward did not like. The degree of superheat attained was in his opinion too high in that heat was thrown away in the exhaust, but from a practical maintenance point of view the design was such that the upper elements could not be removed for inspection or cleaning without withdrawing the lower ones first. So as far as Churchward was concerned the Schmidt superheater was out, regardless of what so many other railways were doing. His interest in American practice then came to the fore, and in May 1907 the last of the new Stars of that year, No 4010 *Western Star* was built new with the Cole type of superheater. The attraction of this apparatus was that the elements were straight, and any one could be removed without disturbing any of the others, but the actual design of the elements was unacceptable at Swindon, and work began on a design of their own, in which the details were due to Messrs C. C. Champeney and G. H. Burrows. There were three stages in this development; the Swindon No 1 type was tried on No 4011 *Knight of the Garter* in 1908, and the No 2 on No 2922 *Saint Gabriel* later that year. The final version, the No 3, was introduced in 1909. Its first application on a passenger locomotive was on the 4-cylinder 4-6-0 No 4021 *King Edward*, the first of that new series and the only one to have a superheater when new. No 4021 was completed in June, but it had been preceded by a 2-8-0, No 2808, in March of that year, with an apparatus of slightly different dimensions. So far as 4-4-0s were concerned, Bulldog No 3728 (afterwards 3438) was the first to have a superheater on the

No 2 boiler, in August 1909, and the first on a No 4 boiler was on No 3478 (afterwards 3835) *County of Devon*, in October 1909. The application to the three types of boiler was therefore almost simultaneous.

This superheater was designed to provide for ready inspection and cleaning, both for the ordinary flue tubes and the superheater, and to permit of the removal of any group of elements without disturbing the rest. Another point not generally appreciated was that by so shaping the header the velocity of the steam was made practically constant in its passage through the superheater, thus avoiding the risk of over-heating locally. Those improvements were obtained by arranging the vertical hollow members above and below the header, instead of below only, and a subsidiary advantage resulted from this arrangement, because it permitted the inclusion of a row of ordinary flue tubes between the two rows of larger tubes containing the superheater. This enabled greater strength to be retained in the tubeplate than where rows of large tubes are adjacent. Each of the large flues

One of the final series of Bulldogs, still carrying original number, but with superheater and top feed: No 3743 (later 3453) *Seagull. (W. J. Reynolds)*

contained a set of six steam tubes arranged in horseshoe fashion, held in position by plates placed at suitable intervals. The plates served to assist in retarding and mixing the gases of combustion in their passage. The six steam tubes formed three distinct loops in parallel, and not in series as in the Schmidt. The steam travel was thus shorter, and the degree of superheat not so high. This latter was of course a major design feature of Churchward's practice, in which he aimed to avoid throwing away heat, as waste, in the exhaust. The original arrangement provided for 14 large flues on the No 1 and No 4 boilers, and for 12 on the No 2; this meant there were 84 elements on the former and 72 on the latter, providing heating surfaces of 260, 216 and 170sq ft on types 1, 4 and 2 respectively.

The Swindon No 3 superheater gave steam

Badminton No 3299 (later 4107) *Alexander Hubbard*, superheated and with top feed. *(British Railways)*

temperatures of about 550°F against 380°F, which is the temperature of formation of dry saturated steam at a pressure of 200lb/sq in or 390°F at 225lb/sq in. The increased potential of superheated steam is most clearly shown by comparison of the volumes per pound, namely 2.3cu ft saturated, against 2.9cu ft superheated to 550°F, an increase of 26 per cent. It was this fundamental point that led many locomotive engineers to increase the diameter of the cylinders of superheated locomotives in relation to those of similar saturated designs. With the Schmidt superheater, as it came to be used on the London & North Western Railway, with steam temperatures of about 650°F, the volume of a pound of steam was about 3.25cu ft, or 43 per cent greater than of saturated steam. This led some engineers to reduce boiler pressures, to reduce boiler maintenance charges, as well as to increase cylinder diameters. On the Great Western Churchward did neither; he kept boiler pressure and cylinder diameter the same, and in actual performance on the road there was less *apparent* difference between the work of saturated and superheater locomotives than on any other British railway.

Referring again to the construction of the Swindon No 3 superheater, the header itself consisted of two distinct chambers, one for saturated and one for superheated steam, and a number of passages at the back of the header

Atbara class 4-4-0 No 4138 *White*, fitted with the Westinghouse brake. *(Author's collection)*

connected those two chambers, thus to establish communication with the steam tubes, causing circulation of saturated steam through the superheater. At opposite ends of the header there were connections to the boiler and to the cylinders, so that steam passed from the regulator into the header, through the super-heater tubes, and thence to the cylinders. Covering the portion of the superheater that projected into the smokebox was a casing provided with a damper for regulating the proportion of the furnace gases that passed through the superheater flues and the ordinary tubes respectively. This damper was closed normally, but was opened by a small cylinder fixed on the outside of the smokebox, which was in turn supplied with steam only when the regulator was opened, and steam therefore passing through the superheater tubes. At a later stage, as will be mentioned in subsequent chapters of this book, the superheaters used on the No 2 standard boilers were reduced to only six sets of elements, instead of the original twelve.

Before setting out details of the many variations of superheaters used on the No 2 and No 4 standard boilers covering the 4-4-0 passenger locomotives, it is interesting to study the chronology of the fitting of superheaters, which came so rapidly after the design of the Swindon No 3 type had been largely finalised. The totals for the years 1909 to 1913 were as shown opposite.

This was indeed a remarkable achievement in

The first 4-4-0 to have a taper boiler: *Mauritius* as renumbered 3705 and superheated. *(W. J. Reynolds)*

4-4-0 LOCOMOTIVE SUPERHEATED

Year	County	City	Arm-strong	Bad-minton	Flower	Bull-dog	Total
1909	2	—	—	—	—	1	3
1910	13	4	—	—	26	52	95
1911	7	14	3	10	12	53	99
1912	6	3	—	6	9	29	53
1913	2	—	1	4	3	11	21
TOTAL	30	21	4	20	50	146	271

so short a time, and by the end of the year 1913 only nine Bulldogs remained to be equipped to complete the above six classes. The conversion of no fewer than 271 locomotives in a space of only four years was a mark of the confidence felt in the efficiency of the No 3 Swindon superheater; the figures quoted refer only to the domeless-boilered 4-4-0s. The 10-wheel locomotives originally built to use saturated steam were being similarly treated at the same time.

In the same period a start was made in superheating the domed-boiler Duke class. Seven of them were converted in 1911, using the 2-row type with 12 large flues, as on the No 2 standard domeless boilers, but after another three had been treated in 1912 this programme slowed down to a mere trickle.

Associated with the development of superheating was the introduction of piston valves. Churchward began experimenting with these at an early date, and again he was much attracted to contemporary American designs. It was the

semi-plug valve among these that was eventually chosen for standardisation, 10in diameter for the standard 2-cylinder classes with 18in cylinders, as on the Counties. In this design the rings were pressed outwards to the liners by steam pressure, and locked in position there by the wedge rings, so that they automatically adjusted themselves to the bore and floated in it with very little friction. It was a good production job for the works, and required little in the way of hand fitting. Nevertheless they were an assembly rather than a fitting job in the works consisting of a lot of bits and pieces—rather complicated—and decidedly heavier than the simple plug type of piston valve with a series of narrow Ramsbottom rings, which in later years was found so effective by Stanier on the London Midland & Scottish Railway. The British patent rights of the American semi-plug valve were however acquired by the GWR, and it became a Swindon standard from 1910. In due course an 8in diameter version was produced for the smaller locomotives and this was standardised from 1914 onwards on Cities, Flowers, Bulldogs and so on.

The Counties had the standard 18in diameter piston, as shown in the accompanying drawing. It was a very simple design, of box type, with flat sides and cored out to form internal ribs. The piston rod was screwed into the head with a 1 in 48 taper thread until a specified torque was attained. Then the projecting end of the thread was turned flush with the flat face of the piston and a grub screw inserted, half in the rod and half in the head. This design, with flat-sided pistons, simplified the design of the cylinder covers which were also flat internally. The drawing shows the later arrangement of piston rings. At first two rings 1¼in wide were tried, but these did not prove satisfactory, due to breakages and heavy wear. Then two ⅝in wide rings were fitted side by side in the 1¼in wide channels. These were a slight improvement, but

it was later found that the arrangement illustrated was better still, with two rings only. These were then made ¾in wide. These features of detail were all incorporated on the County class, in common with all the other standard 2-cylinder classes.

The valve setting on the Stephenson link motion of the Counties has been described in Chapter One of this book. It gave a tremendous 'punch' when getting away from rest, and when climbing a heavy gradient, but in actual practice it was found that with any cut-off longer than about 40 per cent the explosive-like exhaust beats disturbed the firebed to such an extent as

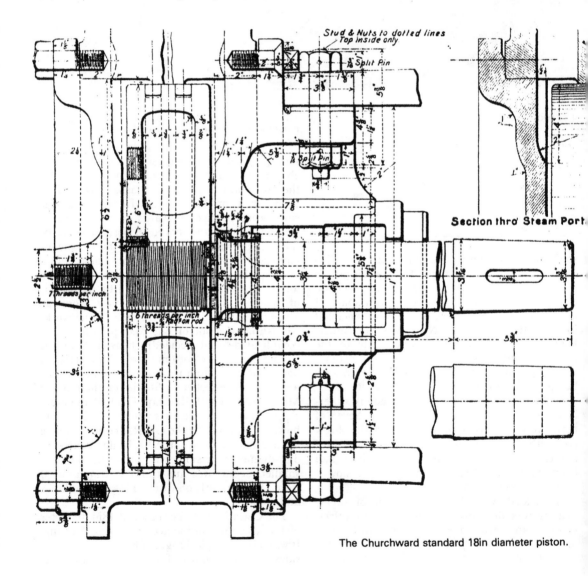

The Churchward standard 18in diameter piston.

No 3815 *County of Hants,* as superheated and fitted with top feed. *(Real Photographs Co Ltd)*

to produce 'holes', with the resultant drop in steam pressure. Churchward, as was his wont, learned of this first-hand from his constant contact with the locomotive running inspectors, and his first thought was to impose a reservoir of some kind between the cylinders and the blastpipe—a kind of silencer to soften and prolong the beat. As an experiment, an extempore modification was made to the standard cylinder and half-saddle casting, opening-out the cored steam passage to make an internal cavity, closing in on the outside by fitting appropriate plates and sealing up to make steam-tight joints. A locomotive was prepared for test, and everyone was very surprised to find that the internal reservoir did not make the slightest difference! So the drawing office had to think again. It was recalled that locomotives maintained from Wolverhampton had an exhaust relief valve below the cylinders, but the objection to it was that it was operated at will by the driver, and in 20th-century conditions, it was felt essential to have something that was automatic. Then the suggestion was put forward of a dead-weight, directly-loaded valve as used on the safety-valves of certain stationary boilers, and this was eventually developed into the well-known jumper ring on the blastpipe. In this simple, but ingenious device the blastpipe was surrounded by a loose cylindrical casting. It was made of

larger diameter than the top, and included an annular space that communicated with the exhaust steam through a number of holes set radially at some distance below the top of the blastpipe. Steam could not escape downwards because of a sealing lip, but when the locomotive was working hard steam entering the annular space in the jumper cap lifted it, and escaped at the top, thereby relieving the force of the blast. Stops limited the upward lift. It was tested in service, and the weight of the cap was adjusted until it did not lift at any cut-off less than 40 per cent. It then became a standard fitting on all modern GWR locomotives.

The last feature that put the finishing touch on the Counties, in common with all the other standard designs was that of boiler feed. In common with most locomotives of the early 20th-century, Swindon types were fed through the conventional clackboxes, or non-return valves. On some classes, like the Dean 7ft 8in 4-2-2 singles its exterior was a spectacular and highly-burnished fitting on the side of the boiler just in rear of the smokebox. With the introduction of the domeless Belpaire boilers on the inside-cylinder 4-4-0s the clacks were placed on the underside of the barrel, and had a diverting arrangement that caused the incoming water to flow towards the firebox. This was not a

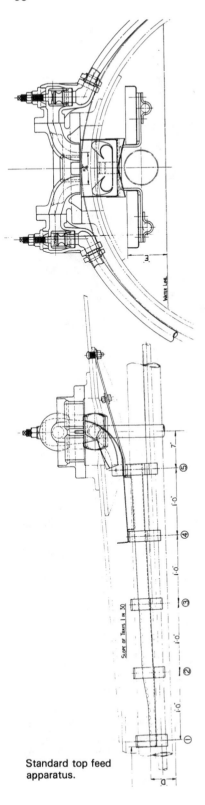

Standard top feed
apparatus.

satisfactory arrangement, and led to pitting and corrosion of the diverting shield. Churchward was aware that a system of top feed had been tried in France in 1890, without any conspicuous success, however. The principle was studied anew at Swindon, and some very careful trials made to determine shape and inclination of the proposed trays to secure an absolutely even distribution. An experimental model was set up, quite apart from a boiler, and a metered supply of water to represent an injector feed was passed into a tray, the shape and inclination of which could be adjusted. The inflowing water fell on the perforated trays, and entered the boiler water in the form of a spray. The meeting point of the hot and cold water was on the trays. There the worst pitting took place, and the trays could be readily removed for replacement. The accompanying drawing shows the arrangement as applied to the standard No 1 and No 4 boilers. Once a device was perfected no time was lost in getting it on to the locomotives and by the end of 1911 no fewer than 400 had been fitted.

The only 4-4-0s built new with superheaters, jumper ring on the blastpipe, and top feed were the final batch of Counties, Nos 3821-30, completed at Swindon between December 1911 and February 1912. In the erecting shop they followed immediately after the first 20 of the new standard moguls. The new Counties could be readily distinguished from the earlier ones from the more shapely form of the running plate at the smokebox and at the cab, and by the tidier arrangement of the reversing rod from the screw reverser. Their names and numbers were:

3821 *County of Bedford*
3822 *County of Brecon*
3823 *County of Carnarvon*
3824 *County of Cornwall*
3825 *County of Denbigh*
3826 *County of Flint*
3827 *County of Gloucester*
3828 *County of Hereford*
3829 *County of Merioneth*
3830 *County of Oxford*

I was always puzzled why the Hornby model railway firm chose No 3821 for their 'O' gauge model of a County—the only one of the whole 40 with which the Great Western had no physical or traffic connection!

At the end of 1912 the great renumbering plan was put into effect. Prior to that, as the first volume of this book has borne witness, the numbering of the standard gauge 4-4-0s, in

First of the 1911 batch: No 3821 *County of Bedford*.
(British Railways)

keeping with many other groups of Great Western locomotives, was by batches rather than by continuity of class. It was not as haphazard as the time-honoured 'system' of Crewe on the LNWR, but with the desire to impose a unified power classification system on the GWR some revision was necessary. So from 1913 onwards the Bulldogs became the 3300 class; the Flowers incorporating the Badmintons, Atbaras, Armstrongs and Flowers proper, became the 4100 class; the Cities became 3700, and the Counties the 3800 class. Except for the Counties 3801-3830, every locomotive in the above classes was renumbered.

Complete details are given in the case histories at the end of this book, but so far as the Flowers were concerned the 4100 series began with the Badmintons, continued through the Atbaras (omitting the ten locomotives rebuilt with No 4 boilers), and then the Flowers. The four Armstrongs were not added to the class and renumbered until they were rebuilt with piston valves and 6ft 8½in coupled wheels. The City or 3700 class began with the ten rebuilt Atbaras and continued with the Cities proper. In the County class the pioneer, No 3473, was renumbered 3800 and became the class leader, while Nos 3474 to 3482 became 3831-3839. The summary of the 6ft 8½in classes was:

Class	Old Numbers	New Numbers
4100	3292-3311	4100-4119
	3373-3399	4120-4145 *
	3410-3412	4146-4148
	16	4169
	14	4170
	7	4171
	8	4172
3700	3400-3409	3700-3709
	3433-3442	3710-3719
3800	3473	3800
	3474-3482	3831-3839

* No 3382 scrapped — not replaced

The Bulldog renumbering was more complicated, because of the inclusion in the class of 20 locomotives that originally were built as Dukes. These were not a continuous block of numbers in the first place, but came from a diversity of batches. As renumbered, these 20 locomotives became the first batch of Bulldogs, namely Nos 3300 to 3319. After that the Avalons, Camels and the Bulldogs proper followed in the numerical sequence of their numbers, thus:

New Numbers	Old Numbers
3320-3360	3332-3372
3361-3380	3413-3432
3381-3410	3443-3472
3411-3455	3701-3745

The Dukes remained the 3252 class, beginning with *Duke of Cornwall*, but were numbered consecutively up to 3291, filling in the blanks left by the transfer of 20 locomotives to the Bulldog class. The original numbering was 3252 to 3291, and 3312 to 3331.

Apart from the renumbering, the modernisation of the 4-4-0 locomotive stud since 1909 had been remarkable. It was all the more so having regard to the big-engine policy currently being pursued. One might have imagined that while increasing the stock of 4-cylinder 4-6-0s from 20, at the beginning of 1909 to 60 at the end of 1914, and while adding 25 more 2-cylinder 4-6-0s, the lesser lights might have been left to themselves, especially since none of them were really old. It is revealing to compare what happened on the GWR in the momentous five years 1910 to 1914 with contemporary events on the other companies that could be included in the 'biggest five' of the English railway, size being reckoned in terms of total revenue. The Midland with its locomotive department under pressure from an iron-fisted general manager was virtually stagnant. The Lancashire & Yorkshire was still involved in comparing the merits of compounding and superheating, and running its principal trains with some strikingly ineffective 4-6-0s. The North Eastern was beginning to equip its smaller and older passenger locomotives with superheaters, and even on the London & North Western, with its massive yearly programmes of new building at Crewe, C. J. Bowen Cooke had to go, cap-in-hand as it were, to higher authority before he was permitted to indulge in the extra expense of fitting his locomotives with superheaters. Churchward, on the other hand, had completely ridden out the storm over the costs of his department. The spectacular results of the locomotive interchange trials of 1910 had so vindicated his policies that he was able to continue with no let or hindrance. By the end of 1914 he had no fewer than 400 superheater passenger locomotives on the road, 285 of which were of the 4-4-0 type. This did not include the few Dukes that had also been equipped by this time.

It is interesting to review the overall scene on the GWR in the years just before World War I, because it might be questioned whether the superheating of such a large number of relatively small and older locomotives was justified—despite Churchward's drive and enthusiasm. Actually he had in mind to replace the entire double-frame stud, Atbaras, Bulldogs and the Aberdare 2-6-0 goods locomotives as early as 1910, despite the fact that the most recent of the Bulldog and the Flower series were then no more than two or three years old.

Bournemouth-Newcastle express (GCR stock) passing Tilehurst, with Badminton class 4-4-0 No 4102 *Blenheim*. *(M. W. Earley)*

Having completed the designs for the range of standard main line locomotives, or so it had then appeared, Churchward felt the need to apply a similar process to the locomotives working on secondary routes. The Great Western had the greatest route mileage of any of the English companies of that time, and the economics of working the very numerous secondary lines was an important consideration at a time when the price of coal was constantly rising. His first intention was to replace the double-frame classes with new single-frame designs, still with inside cylinders, but with 10in diameter piston valves and the standard setting of the Stephenson link motion giving long valve travel. The 10in piston valves located above the cylinders could not be got in without encroaching upon the smokebox and the proposal lapsed. Development of the Aberdares later took the form of the celebrated 43XX 2-6-0 with standard 18in × 30in outside cylinders, but the existing 4-4-0s were modernised, rather than replaced.

In 1910-14 the needs for second-line passenger locomotives were far from confined to the branch and country routes. Two new main lines had recently been opened. In 1908 the new sections linking-up to make a through route between Birmingham and Bristol brought the GWR into direct competition with the Midland on a service that the latter company had enjoyed as a monopoly for very many years; in 1910 the Ashendon-Aynho cut-off line opened the new short route to Birmingham from Paddington, and allowed the GWR to run on equal terms with the LNWR in a highly competitive service. The travelling public is always inclined to be conservative in its habits, and a London businessman who for many years had made for

A Bulldog, in the unlined green style: No 3403 (originally 3465) *Trinidad. (British Railways)*

Euston and a particular train when bound for Birmingham would not readily try Paddington as an alternative, despite the attractive publicity given to the new route opened in 1910. In more of a family vein I remember how my own mother preferred dingy, old-fashioned New Street for any sort of journey from Birmingham. So, in launching the new routes against solid well entrenched traditions the GWR had to ensure frequent, fast, and convenient trains, and an impeccable standard of punctuality. Patronage was at first meagre, and coach formations accordingly small. On the Paddington-Birmingham route extensive use was made of slip coaches to avoid intermediate stops, and some of the most competitive trains ran with no more than four coaches over lengthy sections of their routes. Although Saint class 4-6-0s were used on some of the Birmingham trains the 4-4-0s were ideal for these fast lightly-loaded runs. Nothing larger was in any case permitted on the Birmingham-Bristol run, over which running powers on the Midland part of the line between Standish Junction and Yate were exercised. For a time, however, the Midland Railway did make an exception in favour of the French compound Atlantics, which were occasionally used.

Two other important express routes remained exclusive 4-4-0 preserves, at any rate up to the end of 1914; these were the Oxford, Worcester & Wolverhampton line, and the North to West route from Shrewsbury and Hereford through the Severn Tunnel to Bristol. Both enjoyed a considerably more lavish service in those pre-war years than anything subsequently run, and a considerable stud of 4-4-0 locomotives of both inside- and outside-cylinder types was kept active. At the same time it must be appreciated that the utilisation of locomotives was then far less intense than it subsequently became. A single return trip from Wolverhampton to Paddington and back, sometimes outward via Birmingham and back via Worcester was considered the very maximum. In Cornwall, until the introduction of the 43XX Moguls, the Dukes and the Bulldogs had the job to themselves. In South Wales west of Cardiff there was still, in 1914, very little penetration by 4-6-0s. There was thus a wide, diverse and important field of activity for the full 4-4-0 range, and Churchward's policy of modernisation on such a thorough and comprehensive scale was amply justified. Until the continuance of war conditions made certain economies necessary, the 4-4-0s of all classes were finished in the panoply of old, with full lining-out, polished brass safety-valve covers, and copper-capped chimneys. The large diameter variety of these latter became general until war conditions demanded the suppression of spit-and-polish.

May I conclude this chapter with a few personal memories. From 1910 my home was at Mortimer Common, and I held a season ticket

A Bulldog, in the post-war style developed at some sheds: plain green, but copper-capped chimney, and polished safety-valve cover—No 3407 *Madras. (W. J. Reynolds)*

between Mortimer station and Reading. Several times, too, the family spent holidays at Weymouth. The Channel Islands boat trains were sometimes worked by Counties, but otherwise Bulldogs and Flowers predominated, and I remember so well how the Great Western locomotives outshone those of the London & South Western, which of course were equally numerous on the ground at Weymouth. Most of the through London trains then changed locomotives at Reading. They would be brought down from Paddington by one of the domeless-boilered Barnum 2-4-0s, and the Bulldog would then take over at Reading. I particularly remember on the Weymouth run No 3445 (later 3383) *Ilfracombe* and No 3742 (later 3452) *Penguin*, together with Atbara No 3392 (later 4138) *White*. Also I recall seeing several of those actually named after flowers, but at this distance in time I cannot remember individual examples.

CHAPTER FOUR

PERFORMANCE—MAINLY ON NEW ROUTES

The inauguration of the new through service between Birmingham and Bristol in 1908 had been the subject of acute controversy, and eventually litigation between the GWR and the Midland. Although holding running powers over the latter line between Bristol and Standish Junction, near Stonehouse, the GWR wished to use them only north of Yate, entering upon Midland metals by the sharply-curved link from Westerleigh West Junction. The Midland argued that this connection should be used only by trains diverging again at Berkeley Road South Junction, and going thence over the Severn Bridge. If the line to Standish was to be used, Great Western trains must use the Midland line throughout from Bristol, and pay the appropriate toll charges. The Great Western took the case to the courts, but judgment was given in favour of the Midland. Because of this dispute the new GWR service got off to a bad start, with only one through train in each direction, between Wolverhampton and Penzance. The inaugural train in each direction was worked by the then new Flower class 4-4-0 No 4101 *Auricula*, but no actual running details were published. By the following summer, however, the dispute had been resolved, and the Great Western route via Filton and Westerleigh West Junction was being used by three trains in each direction. The Bristol departures were 9.05am Bristol to Birkenhead, 12.23pm Weston-super-Mare to Wolverhampton, attaching through carriages from Kingswear and Ilfracombe at Bristol, and the 'Penzance', leaving Bristol at 4.45pm.

It was not a route over which high average speeds could be expected. It began with the stiff climb up the 1 in 75 of Filton bank, and then came the very severe slowing round the connecting curve from Westerleigh to Yate. Good speed could certainly be made over the Midland line to Standish Junction, but there was another severe speed restriction there to cross over on to Great Western metals, and speed had hardly been regained from this when more slow running was required over the Gloucester avoiding line, terminating at Engine Shed Junction. All trains by the new route stopped at Cheltenham, Malvern Road, so that the speed restrictions over the junctions at each end of that station were of no account so far as overall times were concerned. In the circumstances it was not surprising that the best time that could be scheduled between Bristol Stapleton Road and Cheltenham, 43.1 miles, was exactly one hour.

The table on page 44 gives summary details of five runs over this section. Because of the initial difficulties it was rarely possible to pass Yate in much under 20 minutes, though of course on the first run the lightly-loaded Bulldog, No 3414 *A. H. Mills* was able to make easy work of Filton bank. Great Western trains did not often get through the Gloucester area without some delay, no doubt through Midland trains being given preference at the various junctions. At that time also the line between Gloucester and Cheltenham was only double-tracked, so forming something of a bottleneck. On the second run *County of Cardigan* made the best start of the County class up Filton bank, but neutralised it by some very slow down-hill running after Yate. The similarly-loaded *County of Middlesex* and *County of Stafford* ran very much harder. The latter in particular reached a

GWR BRISTOL (STAPLETON ROAD) - CHELTENHAM

Run No:		1	2	3	4	5
Locomotive No:		3414	3812	3800	3837	3828
Locomotive Name:		A.H. Mills	County of Cardigan	County of Middlesex	County of Stafford	County of Hereford
Load, tons		80	175	175	180	295
Distance Miles		Actual min sec	Actual min sec	Actual min sec	Actual min sec	Actual min sec
0.0	STAPLETON ROAD	0 00	0 00	0 00	0 00	0 00
3.2	Filton	6 20	7 30	8 05	7 45	9 25
—		—	—	—	—	sigs
10.3	Yate	17 40	18 45	20 15	20 00	22 35
17.0	Charfield	24 45	25 15	26 40	27 00	30 45
24.6	Coaley	31 45	33 05	33 20	33 25	37 15
—		sigs	—	—	—	—
30.1	Standish Junc	38 05	39 45	39 10	38 40	42 40
—		sigs	sigs	sigs	sigs	—
37.3	Engine Shed Junc	sigs	48 30	49 15	—	50 25
43.1	CHELTENHAM (Midland Road)	53 05	56 35	57 25	57 35	58 45
Average speed, mph Charfield-Coaley		65.2	58.1	68.5	71.0	62.8

maximum of 75mph at the foot of the Charfield bank, and sustained speed so well over the slightly undulating stretch that follows as to average 71mph from Charfield to Coaley. Nevertheless, in the years between 1909 and 1914 when these runs were made, loads of 175 to 180 tons would have been considered mere featherweights compared to those hauled by 4-4-0 locomotives of comparable tractive power at that time. *County of Hereford* had a harder task on the 'Penzance', and made distinctly heavy weather of Filton bank. The check approaching Yate was not serious, and with no more than moderate speed down the Charfield bank, and no checks around Gloucester time was kept with just over a minute in hand. Had the locomotives on the three preceding runs been able to make comparable times north of Standish Junction, their overall times from Stapleton Road to Cheltenham would have been 55¾, 55¼, and 54¾ minutes respectively.

The continuation work of the same four County class locomotives from Cheltenham to Stratford-on-Avon is shown in the next table, and here their running is compared to that of two Atbaras, both of which had been renumbered at the time of making these runs. The climb from Cheltenham to Gotherington is not severe. After a sharp, but short gable, the inclination is 1 in 200 except for one mile at 1 in 150. After that comes an almost level table land to Winchcombe, followed by a generally downward tendency almost to Stratford. The only appreciably adverse stretch is a mile at 1 in 202-156 to Honeybourne East Junction. There was nominally a slight speed restriction between the west and east junctions, but in these early days of the route it was interpreted somewhat

GWR CHELTENHAM-STRATFORD-ON-AVON

Run No:		1	2	3	4	5	6
Locomotive No:		4142	4145	3812	3800	3837	3828
Locomotive Name:		Brisbane	Dunedin	County of Cardigan	County of Middlesex	County of Stafford	County of Hereford
Load tons		110	195	175	175	180	295
Distance Miles		Actual min sec	Actual min sec	Actual min sec	Actual min sec	Actual min sec	Actual min sec
0.0	CHELTENHAM (Malvern Road)	0 00	0 00	0 00	0 00	0 00	0 00
5.6	Gotherington	7 20	—	8 35	8 35	—	9 55
9.0	Winchcombe	10 50	13 05	12 30	12 40	11 35	14 15
—		—	—	pws	—	—	—
16.1	Broadway	17 00	—	20 55	19 25	17 35	21 00
21.1	Honeybourne East Junc	21 00	24 40	25 25	23 55	22 30	25 35
26.1	Milcote	25 45	—	29 55	28 35	—	30 10
29.1	STRATFORD-ON-AVON	29 15	33 55	33 15	31 55	31 40	33 35
Average speed, mph, Broadway-Honeybourne		75.0	—	66.8	66.8	63.3	65.7

No 3801 *County Carlow* on West of England to Wolverhampton express near Wood End. *(L & GRP)*

liberally. Drivers of the County class locomotives, running easily with their light loads, would allow the adverse gradient to reduce their speed sufficiently without the need for shutting off steam. This was certainly not the case on the first run in the table, with Atbara No 4142 *Brisbane*. After having sailed merrily up to Gotherington with the light load, a tremendous spurt was put on down to Honeybourne. The average speed of 75mph from Broadway must have involved a maximum little short of 80mph before the Honeybourne slack.

Schedule time for the 29.1 miles from Cheltenham to Stratford was 35 minutes, and this was more than maintained on all runs. It is a pity that more detail is not available of the second Atbara run, with a load of nearly 200 tons, because the initial climbing was little below the standard of the Counties. On the sixth run *County of Hereford* with the 295-ton load continued to do steady timekeeping work, without any exceptional downhill speed. It is clear from these runs that except for an occasional summer outing, when the traffic was above normal, one would not seek out this route to see the County class being really exerted.

By far the most interesting part of the journey from Bristol to Birmingham was that over the North Warwickshire line, from Stratford-on-Avon to its junction with the north main line at Tyseley. On this there is first of all a sharp 1½ mile ascent at 1 in 75 to Wilmcote, and then after running easily over the Bearley Junctions comes the nine-mile ascent, mostly at 1 in 150 up to Earlswood Lakes. This could be a real grind, particularly in later years when the locomotive of the up 'Penzance' would be working through from Paignton to Wolverhampton. The Castles on this double-home duty worked the Torbay section of the train to Exeter, where it was combined with the Cornish section but in the days when the Counties were on the job locomotives were changed at Bristol. The slightly falling gradient for nearly a mile after Bearley North Junction enabled something of a run to be taken at the long bank. The gradient eases from 1 in 150 to 1 in 181 in the last two miles, to be followed by a gentle descent to the Tyseley junctions.

In the table of six runs between Stratford and Birmingham City No 3708 *Killarney* made short work of the bank with its light train, averaging no less than 57mph between Henley-in-Arden and Earlswood Lakes. Flower No 4157 *Lobelia* also ran smartly, but so far as the inside-cylinder locomotives were concerned, it was No 3711 *City of Birmingham* that claimed the honours, with

GWR STRATFORD-ON-AVON - BIRMINGHAM

Run No:		1	2	3	4	5
Locomotive No:		3708	4157	3711	3828	3806
Locomotive Name:		Killarney	Lobelia	City of Birmingham	County of Hereford	County Kildare
Load tons		85	125	170	295	305
Distance Miles		Actual min sec	Actual min sec	Actual min sec	Actual min sec	Actual min sec
0.0	STRATFORD-ON-AVON	0 00	0 00	0 00	0 00	0 00
8.0	Henley-in-Arden	9 45	10 25	11 05	11 10	12 15
14.8	Earlswood Lakes	16 55	18 05	18 35	19 30	20 20
21.7	Tyseley	23 15	24 25	24 50	26 50	26 55
—		pws	sigs	sigs	—	sigs
25.0	BIRMINGHAM (SNOW HILL)	31 05	30 55	33 10	32 10	33 25
Average speed, mph, Henley-Earlswood		57.0	53.3	54.5	48.7	50.3

an average speed of 54.5mph with its load of 170 tons. The Counties however were really showing-off their paces. *County of Hereford* continued the steady work shown throughout from Bristol, while in the final column No 3806 *County Kildare* with a load of 305 tons, although falling behind somewhat in the immediate start from Stratford, made an excellent climb to Earlswood Lakes, and ran so smartly afterwards as to make the good time of 14 minutes 40 seconds over the 13.7 miles from Henley-in-Arden to Tyseley. To those of us

Wolverhampton-South Wales express near Wood End, hauled by No 4120 *Atbara. (L & GRP)*

whose personal recollections of the route are of Castles hauling trains of more than 400 tons these runs with 4-4-0s make so many fascinating period pieces.

Equally so are early records of running on the short route from Paddington to Birmingham via Bicester. Nevertheless, turning through the records of published accounts that appeared at the time, and particularly the writings of Cecil J. Allen in *The Railway Magazine*, it is remarkable to find no reference at all to the part 4-4-0 locomotives played in the inauguration of that notable new service. I suppose it was no more than natural that attention at that time was centred upon the running of Churchward's

Birmingham-Paddington express (via Bicester) near Ruislip: No 3823 *County of Carnarvon*. *(H. Gordon Tidey)*

4-6-0s. Much of it was indeed very impressive, but anyone researching in published records might well gain the impression that the 4-6-0s had the service to themselves from the very outset. From the voluminous books of records so kindly put at my disposal by the late E. L. Bell this was very far from being the case. It was not only that the Flowers, Atbaras and Cities took their turns on the lighter trains, but that the Counties, and sometimes even the inside-cylinder locomotives took turns with the 4-6-0s on the heavier ones, like the sharply booked 9.10am down from Paddington, which included a stop at High Wycombe in the overall time of two hours to Birmingham. On five runs with this train logged by Cecil J. Allen all with 2-cylinder 4-6-0 locomotives, the loads leaving Paddington were 270, 280, 260, 240, and 200 tons, whereas on two runs to be mentioned later County class locomotives on the same train kept time with initial loads of 310 and 275 tons.

It is evident also that a considerable variation in driving standards prevailed. By this I do not mean that there was any laxity in engine management, but that while some crews did all they could to recover time lost by signal and permanent way checks, others would do no more than keep their scheduled point-to-point times on the undelayed sections, and arrive a corresponding amount of time late. This was not peculiar to the new route to Birmingham but characteristic of the great majority of main lines throughout the steam era in Great Britain. So far as the 4-4-0 locomotives are concerned I am only sorry that the early records passed on to me do not include more complete details of the undoubtedly very fine runs by Counties on the

9.10am from Paddington. The table on page 48 sets out details of three runs with inside-cylinder 4-4-0s between Paddington and Leamington. The first of these with the Atbara No 3390 *Terrible*, presented an easy task with a load of no more than 120 tons. Nevertheless some very smart running was made, with an average speed of 62.8mph over the uphill stretch from Denham to Beaconsfield through the Chilterns and of 75mph downhill from Princes Risborough to Ashendon Junction. By that time the train was drawing ahead of schedule and the effort was eased. *City of Birmingham* on the second run, made an extremely vigorous start out of London, and the time of 9 minutes 45 seconds from Northolt to Beaconsfield showed an average speed of no less than 70mph over this level and uphill stretch. With fast work down from Princes Risborough and an average speed of 75mph on to Ashendon Junction, the latter point was passed in the notable time of 46 minutes 5 seconds from Paddington, 57.3mph from the start. This was first-class work from a City class locomotive with a load of 185 tons.

On the third run another of the Cities, still in non-superheated condition, was working a two-hour non-stop from Paddington to Birmingham, and as on the run in the second column, slipping a coach at Banbury. This run was completely undelayed until after Leamington. The climb over the Chilterns was more leisurely, with an average speed of 55.8mph from Denham to Beaconsfield. There was some fast running after

PADDINGTON-LEAMINGTON (via BICESTER)

Run No:		1	2	3
Locomotive No:		3390	3711*	3403
Locomotive Name:		*Terrible*	*City of Birmingham*	*Hobart*
Load tons (to Banbury)		120	185	205
(to Leamington)		120	140	180
Distance Miles		*Actual min sec*	*Actual min sec*	*Actual min sec*
0.0	PADDINGTON	0 00	0 00	0 00
—		pws	—	—
4.6	Park Royal	8 50	—	7 55
10.3	Northolt	14 55	13 10	13 45
14.8	Denham	19 10	—	18 15
21.7	Beaconsfield	25 45	22 55	25 40
26.5	High Wycombe	30 15	28 15	30 05
31.5	Saunderton	37 15	35 10	36 25
34.7	Princes Risboro	40 50	38 30	40 00
40.1	Haddenham	45 15	42 45	44 30
44.2	*Ashendon Junc*	48 25	46 05	47 55
47.4	Brill	51 45	50 10	51 30
53.4	Bicester	57 00	56 15	57 30
—		—	pws	—
57.2	Ardley	61 10	61 40	62 00
—		—	pws	—
62.4	*Aynho Junc*	66 10	67 05	67 40
67.5	BANBURY (slip)	70 35	72 25	73 05
76.2	Fenny Compton	78 25	—	—
81.2	Southam Road	82 25	—	86 15
—		sigs	—	—
87.3	LEAMINGTON	89 55	91 40	91 30
Net times, minutes		86	89½	91½

* later numbering

Saunderton, with an average of 72mph from Princes Risborough to Ashendon. The effort was eased considerably after this, and in the absence of delays there was no particular need for hurry. After passing Leamington on the through line at slightly reduced speed, there was first a rapid recovery in the dip between there and Warwick, and the 6.2 miles up to Hatton, including nearly 4 miles at 1 in 110 took only 7½ minutes. There were both permanent way and signal checks in the concluding stages, but the 17.1 miles from Hatton into Birmingham took no more than 20 minutes 35 seconds and the arrival in Snow Hill station was in 119 minutes 35 seconds from Paddington, an eminently satisfactory run.

I have briefer details of five runs with Counties and heavier loads. No 3818 *County of Radnor* left Paddington with a 280-ton load, on a two-hour non-stop that included slip portions detached at Princes Risborough and Banbury. Because of signal checks it took no less than 50 minutes to pass the first station, and 31 minutes 25 seconds for the 32.8 miles on to Banbury. Continuing then with a load of 190 tons, the 19.8 miles on to Leamington took 18 minutes 40 seconds and the 23.3 miles to Birmingham 26

minutes 35 seconds, a total of 126 minutes 40 seconds from Paddington. By contrast, No 3801 *County Carlow*, more heavily loaded throughout, did some excellent work on the morning train calling intermediately at High Wycombe. With an initial load of 310 tons Northolt was passed in 15 minutes 5 seconds and the ensuing 11.4 miles up to Beaconsfield took only 11 minutes 40 seconds. One would like to see more detail of what must have been a magnificent climb over the Chilterns, but unfortunately no more is available in the contemporary notes at my disposal. High Wycombe was reached in 31 minutes 55 seconds. This train slipped coaches at Bicester and Banbury, reducing the load first to 285 and then to 260 tons. Ashendon Junction, 17.7 miles from the restart, was passed in 20¼ minutes, Bicester 26.9 miles, in 29 minutes 25 seconds, and Banbury 41 miles, in 43 minutes 50 seconds. With the load now reduced to 260 tons there came a stirring finish, with a time of only 17 minutes 35 seconds for the 19.8 miles on to Leamington, and 24 minutes 25 seconds for the last 23.3 miles into Birmingham, including ascent of the Hatton bank, making a total of 85 minutes 50 seconds for the 84.1 miles run non-

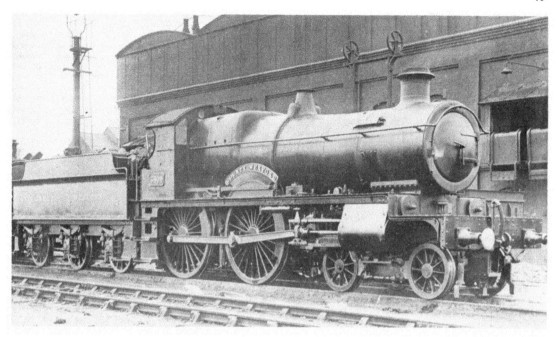

No 3809 *County Wexford* in the plain green of World War I. *(W. J. Reynolds)*

stop from High Wycombe. The total running time from Paddington was thus 118 minutes 45 seconds, giving an average of 56 mph.

No 3830 *County of Oxford*, on the same train but with a load lighter throughout, also did well, with 275 tons to Bicester, 245 tons to Banbury, and only 195 tons onwards to Birmingham. High Wycombe was reached in 30 minutes 50 seconds after which the times from the restart were 29 minutes 50 seconds to Bicester (including 1½ minutes lost by a relaying check), 43 minutes 45 seconds to Banbury, 64¼ minutes to Leamington (again checked by relaying), and 89 minutes 40 seconds into Birmingham. Comparisons may be odious, but in recent years so many derogatory comments have been made by a variety of authors about the County class that I cannot resist setting out the basic features of these two splendid runs alongside the five runs with 2-cylinder 4-6-0s published in *The Railway Magazine* for March 1911. The booked times were 30 minutes start to stop, from Paddington to High Wycombe, which only one of the 4-6-0s managed to keep, and then 89 minutes onwards to Birmingham, on which the heavily-loaded No 3801 *County Carlow* tied with the fastest of all the 4-6-0 runs, on which the load was more than 100 tons less throughout. This train was worked by engines and men from Old Oak

PADDINGTON-BIRMINGHAM — A COMPARISON

Run No:	1	2	3.	3	4	5	6
Locomotive No:	2915	2912	178	2916	2924	3830	3801
Loads: (a)	270	280	260	240	200	275	310
(b)	245	255	235	215	175	245	285
(c)	180	180	180	180	140	195	260
	min sec	min sec	min sec	min sec	min sec	min sec	min sec
Paddington	0 00	0 00	0 00	0 00	0 00	0 00	0 00
High Wycombe	32 25	30 45	31 00	29 45	31 30	30 50	31 55
Banbury	47 45	45 20	46 10	44 05	42 10	43 45	43 50
Leamington	65 50	63 20	64 55	62 25	62 40	64 15	61 45
Birmingham	89 00	88 20	88 45	88 35	89 40	89 40	85 50
Net times, minutes: High Wycombe- Birmingham	87 ½	87	87 ¼	87 ¼	85	86 ¾	85

LEAMINGTON-PADDINGTON (via BICESTER)

Run No:		1	2	3	4	5	6	7	8
Locomotive No:		4110	4106	4110	4106	3818	3819	3829	3814
Locomotive Name:		Petunia	Campanula	Petunia	Campanula	County of Radnor	County of Salop	County of Merioneth	County of Chester
Load, tons:		120	120	135	200	180	180	215	320/240
Distance Miles		Actual min sec	Actual min sec	Actual min sec	Actual min sec	Actual min sec	Actual min sec	Actual min sec	Actual min sec
0.0	LEAMINGTON	0 00	0 00	0 00	0 00	0 00	0 00	0 00	0 00
6.1	Southam Road	8 45	8 50	8 05	9 20	9 30	9 10	8 40	10 25
—		—	pws	pws	pws	—	—	—	pws
11.1	Fenny Compton	13 55	14 30	—	16 20	15 00	14 15	13 25	19 10
19.8	BANBURY	22 25	22 30	23 30	25 25	23 45	22 15	20 50	28 55*
24.9	Aynho Junc	27 05	26 40	27 50	30 00	28 30	26 40	24 50	33 40
30.1	Ardley	32 40	31 30	33 05	35 25	34 25	32 10	29 55	39 05
33.9	Bicester	35 50	34 40	36 20	38 40	37 55	35 30	33 10	42 45
39.9	Brill	40 40	39 45	41 30	43 25	42 55	40 35	38 15	48 35
43.1	Ashendon Junc	44 00	43 00	44 50	46 30	46 20	44 05	41 15	51 55
47.2	Haddenham	47 45	46 45	48 20	50 20	50 05	47 55	45 25	56 00
—		—	—	pws	—	—	—	—	—
52.6	Princes Risborough	53 20	52 15	54 35	55 50	55 25	53 20	50 40	61 35
60.8	High Wycombe	61 55	60 45	62 20	64 15	64 25	62 00	59 20	70 15
65.6	Beaconsfield	67 15	65 55	67 10	70 00	69 50	67 25	64 10	75 35
77.0	Northolt	77 25	—	76 30	79 15	79 30	77 00	73 45	—
82.7	Park Royal	sigs	80 40	81 15	83 50	84 15	81 40	79 35	90 05
—		sigs	sigs	—	sigs	sigs	sigs	sigs	—
87.3	PADDINGTON	93 20	88 45	88 35	92 15	92 40	90 00	89 40	97 00
Net times	minutes	89½	87	86	90¼	91¼	88¾	86½	94
Average Speeds mph									
	Ardley-Haddenham	68.5	67.3	67.3	68.8	65.6	65.3	66.3	60.5
	Beaconsfield-Northolt/Park Royal	67.4	69.6	72.5	74.2	71.2	71.6	66.1	70.8

* Slip coach detached

Common shed, who returned on the 2.45pm up from Birmingham. This latter train was booked to take 28 minutes from Snow Hill to Leamington, make a two-minute stop there, and continue non-stop to Paddington in 95 minutes. A County run on this train is set out in the table on this page. In making these comparisons it must not be imagined that I am inferring that the 2-cylinder 4-6-0 could not have done better; far from it. No one had a higher opinion of them than I have. It is merely that those published details of 1911 did not reveal them as the marvels the accompanying description suggested, and as the only contemporary account of early days on the short route to Birmingham it is only fair to view them in true perspective, particularly as they affect the record of the 4-4-0s. On one of the trains stopping intermediately at Leamington No 3801 County Carlow with a load of 295 tons passed High Wycombe in 31 minutes 35 seconds and then despite one signal check covered the 41 miles on to Banbury in 46 minutes 10 seconds. After this, with load reduced to 260 tons by loss of the slip coach, the concluding 19.8 miles to Leamington, severely delayed, took 21¾ minutes to the stop— total 99½ minutes from Paddington. The last of

the five County runs was on the same train, but very severely delayed. No 3819 County of Salop with an initial load of 240 tons took 36 minutes 50 seconds to pass High Wycombe, but then, with a clear road, covered the ensuing 35.9 miles to Aynho Junction in 38 minutes 25 seconds. A stop had to be made in Banbury station to detach the slip coach, and the rest of the run was completely lacking in enterprise. But work like that on the first run of County Carlow with a really substantial train showed what excellent service these locomotives could provide. The series of up journeys from Leamington to Paddington display equally satisfactory performance.

Flower class locomotives were much in favour in the early days of the accelerated Birmingham service via Bicester, and with light loads they certainly sparkled. The banks could be climbed at relatively high speed, such as the successive times made over the 5.2 uphill miles from Aynho to Ardley, of 5 minutes 35 seconds, 4 minutes 50 seconds, and 5 minutes 15 seconds on the first three runs in the table. In consequence no very high speeds were needed downhill. On the third run Petunia had made an extremely vigorous start up to Southam Road, over 6.1 miles that include 3 miles of 1 in 187 rising. On the fourth run the load of 200 tons told against No 4106 *Campanula* at the start, but this locomotive made the fastest running of all on the descent off the Chiltern Hills, with an average speed of 74.2mph throughout the 17.1 miles from Beaconsfield to Park Royal.

The work of the two Counties with 180-ton loads in columns 5 and 6 was undistinguished, but that of *County of Merioneth* with 215 tons included some of the finest running in the table. For a time this locomotive was driven by a very capable man, J. Moore of Stafford Road shed, Wolverhampton, and as early as Banbury he had drawn well ahead of all other competitors. The average speed on the gentle descent from Fenny Compton to Banbury was 70.5mph, followed by no less than 76.5mph on to Aynho Junction. There had evidently been a considerable reduction over the junction itself, because the speed up to Ardley averaged only a little over 60mph and subsequent speeds were no more than moderate, though drawing eventually well ahead of even time. The last run, with *County of Chester* carried a substantial load as far as Banbury. When the new service was inaugurated several trains southbound from Birmingham carried portions for the old line via Oxford, and slipped these at Banbury. Hindered also by a bad permanent way slowing *County of Chester* made a slow start to Banbury, and running over the Aynho-Ashendon section was not very energetic. There was some smart running

inwards from High Wycombe, and with a clear road from Park Royal into Paddington the train was only two minutes out on the 95-minute schedule. On the other seven runs in this table the schedule was 91 minutes.

Two long non-stop runs on the South Wales service with City class locomotives in their non-superheated condition are worth mention. On the first No 3408 *Killarney* had a moderate load of 180 tons and passed Slough, 18.5 miles, in 20 minutes 20 seconds and averaged 65½mph on to Reading, passed in 36¼ minutes. Good steady work followed, passing Didcot in 52 minutes 20 seconds and Swindon in 76¼ minutes. Time was then well in hand and although the train was close to even time at Badminton, 100 miles, in 100 minutes 5 seconds, the effort was eased thereafter. In the notes available, no details are given of the passage through the Severn Tunnel but Newport, 133.4 miles, was passed in 138¾ minutes and the concluding 11.7 miles into Cardiff occupied 14 minutes 20 seconds to make a total of 153 minutes 5 seconds from Paddington, an average of 56.9mph. A contemporary run with No 3406 *Melbourne* and 190 tons gave an identical time of 76¼ minutes through Swindon, exactly 100 minutes to Badminton, and 138 minutes 40 seconds to a stop at Newport, an average of 57.7mph. West

Newcastle-Bournemouth express (GCR stock) near Pangbourne: No 3827 *County of Gloucester*. *(Locomotive Publishing Co)*

of Cardiff a good run was made non-stop to Landore by Flower class No 4116 *Mignonette*, hauling a load of 265 tons. The 13.6 uphill miles to Llanharan took 20 minutes 50 seconds followed by a smart 6 minutes 40 seconds for the 6.7 miles to Bridgend. The 4.1 miles up to Stormy Siding including 3 miles of 1 in 132-163 were climbed in 5½ minutes, but a fast descent of Pyle bank followed with a time of 7 minutes 20 seconds for the 8 miles on to Port Talbot. Lastly, the 12.1 miles into Landore, with the stiff climb to Skewen following the speed restriction through Neath, took 16½ minutes making a total of 56 minutes 20 seconds for the 44.5 difficult miles from Cardiff.

Despite the steady introduction of more of Churchward's magnificent 4-6-0s there was a continuing and important role for the 4-4-0 locomotives west of Newton Abbot. The Bulldogs in particular, with 5ft 8in coupled wheels, and when fitted with No 2 standard taper boiler carrying a pressure of 200lb/sq in had a nominal tractive effort of 21,000lb though many had pressures of 190lb/sq in and 195lb/sq in. This high tractive effort for a locomotive of no more than moderate size made them ideal for the steeply-graded main line in the West Country. Except between Plymouth and Truro none of the inclines was excessively long, and the locomotives could be pounded uphill for short periods at steam rates that the relatively small boilers could not sustain for any length of time. I have set out first of all details of five runs from Newton Abbot to Plymouth, non-stop in all cases. In studying these, and the loads that were conveyed, it must be added that the down Cornish Riviera Express was allowed 44

minutes from passing Newton Abbot to the stop at Plymouth, North Road, and on that duty the Star class 4-6-0s were limited to a maximum tare load of 288 tons west of Newton Abbot. In the years before the withdrawal of the London-Plymouth non-stop run in January 1917, such a load was very rarely taken. A gross load of about 260 tons was the more normal maximum.

On the first run tabulated *County of Gloucester* had a relatively light load, 155 tons, and about the same as that of the 'Limited' in the first years of its running via Castle Cary. To pass Dainton summit in 7½ minutes involved some good climbing, and a minimum speed of about 22mph on that fearsome last mile up to the tunnel. The descent to Totnes was leisurely. There was, I believe, a speed limit of 40mph imposed throughout between Aller Junction and Ashburton Junction. There certainly was such in my footplating days, but in the years of which I am now writing scant regard was paid to it sometimes, when a driver was in a hurry. *County of Gloucester* was taken vigorously up the Rattery incline, climbing the 4.6 miles from Totnes in 7 minutes 50 seconds and not falling below 30mph at any point, while the more easily graded 4.5 miles to Wrangaton summit took only 5¾ minutes. Having made such good time to this point the rest was easy.

In the second column of the table Bulldog No 3445 *Ilfracombe* did equally well; in fact the start up to Dainton was remarkable, even for a load of no more than 165 tons. Speed had been rapidly worked up to 43mph beyond Aller Junction and the last mile to Dainton box was covered in exactly two minutes. After another gentle descent to Totnes the climb to Rattery

GWR NEWTON ABBOT-PLYMOUTH

Run No:		1	2	3	4	5
Locomotive No:		3827	3445	3340	3282	3365*
Locomotive Name:		County of Gloucester	Ilfracombe	Marazion	Maristow	Plymouth
Load, tons, full		155	165	180	190	355
Distance Miles		Actual Min sec	Actual min sec	Actual min sec	Actual min sec	Actual min sec
0.0	Newton Abbot	0 00	0 00	0 00	0 00	0 00
3.8	Dainton Box	7 30	6 55	8 15	9 00	6 40
8.6	Totnes	13 30	12 55	13 40	14 15	12 35
13.2	Rattery Box	21 20	21 10	22 50	24 00	—
15.5	Brent	24 30	24 20	—	—	24 45
17.7	Wrangaton	27 05	27 00	28 55	30 30	27 20
23.4	Cornwood	—	32 50	—	—	33 35
27.8	Plympton	37 35	37 20	—	—	37 55
—		sigs.	—	—	—	—
31.8	Plymouth (North Road)	42 55	42 20	43 55	45 25	43 15

* Piloted by 4-4-0 No 3319 *Katerfelto*

GWR PLYMOUTH-NEWTON ABBOT

Run No:		1	2	3	4	5
Locomotive No:		3318	3312	3482 †	3348	3827
Locomotive Name:		Jupiter	Bulldog	County of Pembroke	Titan	County of Gloucester
					3265*	3406
					St. Germans	Melbourne
Load, tons full		150	175	195	285	310
Distance Miles		Actual min sec	Actual min sec	Actual min sec	Actual min sec	Actual min sec
0.0	Plymouth (North Road)	0 00	0 00	0 00	0 00	0 00
4.0	Plympton	6 20	5 25	6 05	5 10	6 30
6.7	Hemerdon Box	12 25	12 05	12 45	10 30	13 10
—		—	—	—	11 40	—
8.4	Cornwood	15 00	—	15 25	15 00	—
—		pws	—	pws	—	—
14.1	Wrangaton	23 25	21 05	24 15	22 00	22 50
16.3	Brent	26 00	23 15	26 45	24 20	25 15
18.6	Rattery Box	28 40	25 40	—	—	28 00
23.2	Totnes	34 45	30 35	33 50	31 40	32 45
28.0	Dainton Box	41 50	36 20	41 30	—	39 15
31.8	Newton Abbot	46 55	42 10	47 00	42 55	45 25

* Pilot detached at Hemerdon
† Original numbering

was again good, with a minimum speed only just below 30mph. With no more than moderate speed downhill from Wrangaton, the total time to Plymouth was 42 minutes 20 seconds. On the third run another Bulldog, No 3340 *Marazion*, made a slower ascent to Dainton, falling to 20mph in the summit tunnel, but ran faster down to Totnes, touching 60mph. The ascent of Rattery was again slower, but with brisk running afterwards Plymouth was reached in 43 minutes 55 seconds. In comparison No 3282 *Maristow*, one of the Bulldogs converted from Duke class did somewhat inferior work, though only in a relative sense; it was no mean work for a 4-4-0 locomotive of those proportions to convey nearly 200 tons unassisted over such a road.

On the last run, with a load of 355 tons, another Bulldog No 3365 *Plymouth*, assisted by Duke No 3319 *Katerfelto*, did some splendid work, seeing that a division of the load in relation to the tractive effort of the two locomotives would have given about 165 tons to the Duke and 190 tons to the Bulldog. They made the fastest time of all up to Dainton, and only fell slightly behind the quick times of the first two runs on passing Wrangaton. Taken all round, these five runs show a standard of performance over this difficult route little below that which was then being put up by the 4-6-0s. It is true that the latter rose subsequently to far greater things, but the 4-4-0s in the role of banking engines continued to take a share in the working, giving massive help even to King class when necessary. Some detailed reference to their

A rather shop-soiled *Sir Lancelot*, with coupling rod removed, and showing little sign of colour. *(H. Gordon Tidey)*

work in this respect is contained in a later chapter in this book.

On the up road I have also tabulated five runs. In this direction, of course, it is the ascent of Hemerdon bank coming so soon after the 'cold' start from Plymouth that provided the principal problem. But comparing these runs with some of my own in later years it would seem that the small locomotives made light of it in relation to the loads they hauled. Whereas in more recent times locomotives were taken gently down the steep descent at 1 in 80 past Laira sheds, and round the curves past Tavistock Junction, the drivers of Bulldogs and Counties seemed to throw in all they had—otherwise how could they have made times of less than six minutes over the first four miles to Plympton! On the first run tabulated, however, after a very smart exit from North Road station, *Jupiter* was taken along no more than moderately. Speed reached 60mph at Plympton, and with this relatively light load fell to 18mph at Hemerdon, after two miles up at 1 in 42.

On the second run, No 3312 *Bulldog* went out of Plymouth like a veritable rocket, but the speed fell to 15mph on Hemerdon bank. Fast time was made over the easier upper part of the rise to Wrangaton, averaging nearly 50mph over the last 7.4 miles. The locomotive was also taken fast over the ensuing stretch to Rattery, averaging 59mph from Wrangaton, though the descent of the incline itself was made at moderate speed. But a splendid ascent from Totnes to Dainton followed. I once clocked 4-6-0 No 2921 *Saint Dunstan* over this 4.8 miles in 5 minutes 35 seconds with a load of 190 tons, and thought it would be nearly a record. From the table it will be seen that *Bulldog*, hauling 175 tons, took only 5¾ minutes. By comparison, the work of *County of Pembroke* was quite inferior, particularly on the banks. Its times of 6 minutes 40 seconds from Plympton to Hemerdon, and 7 minutes 40 seconds from Totnes to Dainton

were not in the same class as those of the inside-cylinder locomotives.

On the fourth run another Bulldog, No 3348 *Titan*, with a 285-ton load had a pilot only to Hemerdon—Duke No 3265 *St. Germans*. The two locomotives made the astonishing time of 10½ minutes to the stop at Hemerdon box, having passed Plympton in the nigh-record time of 5 minutes 10 seconds, achieving 67mph. Restarting on its own, *Titan* did splendidly to cover the remaining 25.1 miles to Newton Abbot in 31¼ minutes. Unfortunately the recorder did not take the time at Dainton summit, but to get from Totnes to Newton Abbot in 11¼ minutes, faster even than *Bulldog* on No 2 run, must have involved a mighty dash at Dainton. On the last run, with a 310-ton load, one had the combination of a City and a County, and the work was sound without being anywhere exceptional.

Lastly, I have tabulated a good run west of Plymouth. In the later 1930s the down 'Limited' when calling at Par to detach its Newquay coach was allowed 52 minutes for the 34.7 miles from Plymouth, and with heavy trains this timing was not always strictly observed by Castle class locomotives. The sectional times were then 29 minutes to Liskeard, and 41 minutes to Bodmin Road. On the excellent run tabulated No 3325 *St. Columb* averaged 36mph up the long climb from St. Germans to Doublebois, and ran no more than moderately down the ensuing 9.3

GWR PLYMOUTH-PAR
Load: 215 tons, full
Locomotive: No 3325 *St Columb*

Average Distance Miles		Actual min sec	speed mph
0.0	Plymouth (North Road)	0 00	—
4.2	Saltash	8 40	29.2
9.3	St. Germans	15 15	46.5
17.8	Liskeard	30 30	33.2
21.1	Doublebois	34 55	44.8
26.9	Bodmin Road	41 35	52.3
30.4	Lostwithiel	45 30	53.7
34.7	Par	53 30	—

CHAPTER FIVE

THE CHANGING SCENE—EXTENSIVE WITHDRAWALS

The outbreak of war in August 1914 is a convenient point at which to review Great Western locomotive development as a whole, in the way it came to affect the numerous stud of 4-4-0 passenger locomotives. It was mentioned in Chapter 3 of this book how Churchward had in mind the replacement of the entire stud of double-frame locomotives, 4-4-0s and 2-6-0s alike, but that different policies eventually prevailed, and that all this group were eventually modernised by the addition of superheating. piston valves, and top feed. This did not mean there was no replacement of passenger locomotives. In February 1908 a start had been made with the scrapping of the Dean 7ft 8in 4-2-2s of the 30XX class, and by the end of 1914 only four remained in traffic. In the meantime 76 obsolete singles had been replaced by 95 new 4-6-0s—45 Saints and 50 Stars. The last-built of the latter

took the road in July 1914. At the end of 1914 only one Bulldog remained non-superheated, though substitution of piston valves was not done simultaneously. The dates are given in the case histories of individual locomotives at the end of this book. The superheating of the Duke class was much more gradual. By the end of 1914 only ten of them had been equipped, and no more than three others were superheated during the war years. Furthermore, only four, Nos 3264, 3279, 3282 and 3286 (new numbering) had boiler changes during this same period. From January 1915 the boiler position on the Duke class engines was as overleaf.
The four still carrying the original type of boiler

An official record of the 'plain green' style on a Bulldog: No 3450 *Peacock. (British Railways)*

No 3418 *Sir Arthur Yorke* in plain green but with brass bands on splashers polished. *(British Railways)*

Type of Boiler	Number of locomotives fitted
Flush Belpaire firebox, large dome on back ring	33
Flush round-topped firebox, large dome on back ring (original design)	4
Raised Belpaire firebox, large dome on back ring	1
Raised Belpaire firebox, domeless	2

with round-topped firebox were rebuilt with the flush Belpaire type at various times between 1915 and 1917, thus leaving only three that differed from the rest in having raised Belpaire fireboxes.

By May 1914 Churchward had 60 of the new 43XX class 2-6-0s on the road, but although they were built as an alternative to replacing the

No 3803 *County Cork* (with short safety-valve cover) on special train. *(Real Photographs Ltd)*

Bulldogs and Aberdares it was only in Cornwall that they supplanted the 4-4-0s to any extent. During the first years of World War I an attempt was made to carry on railway business as usual, extending to summer holidays in 1915. Many people who would normally have gone abroad sought out English resorts, with the result that traffic to the West of England was at times exceptionally heavy, and every passenger engine that could turn a wheel was needed. Most of the new Moguls were engaged in fast freight duty, but their speediness made them useful for main line passenger work of a secondary kind. Their takeover from the Bulldogs in Cornwall might have been even more complete had not early experience with them shown that on severely curved track serious flange wear was developing on the leading coupled wheels.

It is interesting to speculate as to how war conditions affected Churchward's standardisation programme. The complete cessation of

passenger locomotive building from July 1914 until after his retirement at the end of 1921 was of course complementary to the gradual withdrawal of train services facilities, and from 1917 onwards of drastic deceleration of schedules. But on certain other British railways beset with very heavy wartime traffic, such as the London & North Western and the Caledonian, construction of passenger locomotives continued, albeit on a reduced scale. On the Great Western I think it is probable that, but for the war, the 40 ageing 4-4-0s of the Duke class would have been scrapped. There were very few routes over which they worked that were not available to Bulldogs, and the latter would have been in course of replacement by the 43XX class. As it was, no more than 100 main line locomotives of a mixed traffic category were built at Swindon in the war years 1915-18, and of those 20 went abroad in the service of the Railway Operating Division of the British Army. Railway enthusiasts would agree that one of the few good things that came out of World War I was that it prolonged the life of the Dukes, and that afterwards conditions arising out of the Grouping in 1922 prolonged it still further, as will be told in the following chapter.

Wartime conditions threw a very heavy traffic on to the North to West route via Shrewsbury and Hereford. This was partly due to travel between the industrial districts of South Wales and Lancashire, and in this traffic the County class 4-4-0s were called upon to play a leading part. It is indeed doubtful if Churchward, including an 'American' among his standard locomotives of 1901 as a *riposte* to 'Old Webb' envisaged such loads as they were called upon to haul in 1915-18. 4-6-0 locomotives of the Saint class were not allocated to this route until 1916, so far as I can trace. Even then the Counties were often requisitioned for heavy duty. I have set out in the accompanying table details of six runs between Pontypool Road and Hereford, all with 4-4-0s. The loads were often at their heaviest over this steeply-graded section, because of the conveyance of through carriages from South Wales to Birmingham on trains from Bristol and the west to Liverpool and Manchester. The first two runs were on trains that were a relic of pre-war practice, neither stopping at Pontypool Road. The first was on a through express from South Wales to Birmingham, obviously uneconomic to run in wartime, and withdrawn in 1917. The second was on a train that combined its West of England and South Wales portions at Maindee North Junction. The times given in the table are those from passing Pontypool Road at reduced speed.

The Bulldog, No 3323 *Etona*, made easy work of the 130-ton load, and with speeds of 70mph before Penpergwm and 74mph at Pontrilas achieved the excellent start-to-stop time of 40½ minutes over the 33.4 miles from Pontypool Road to Hereford. It includes the severe climb to Llanvihangel summit on which the minimum speed on 1 in 95 was 31mph and a slow run in from Red Hill Junction. So far as individual locomotives are concerned I am using the new post-1912 numbers from now onwards. On the second run *Ottawa*, which despite the name was not a City in the Great Western sense, but a Bulldog, did very much inferior work with a train, which even after the combining of the two sections at Maindee loaded to no more than 225 tons.

Quite contrasting was the work of No 3718 *City of Birmingham* with a 230-ton load. The

GWR PONTYPOOL ROAD-HEREFORD						
Run No:		1	2	3	4	5
Locomotive No:		3323	3399	3718	38XX	4119
Locomotive Name:		Etona	Ottawa	City of Winchester	—	Wynnstay*
Load, tons full		130	225	230	275	310
Distance Miles		Actual min sec	Actual min sec	Actual min sec	Actual min sec	Actual min sec
0.0	Pontypool Road	0 00†	0 00†	0 00	0 00	0 00
6.7	Penpergwm	7 05	9 03	9 00	8 40	8 45
9.4	Abergavenny	10 40	12 55	12 25	12 20	12 13
13.4	Llanvihangel	18 05	21 30	19 40	20 45	20 10
20.9	Pontrilas	24 55	29 40	27 35	28 20	28 53
30.1	Red Hill Junc	35 35	—	38 00	sigs	—
33.4	Hereford	40 30	47 40	sig stop	47 20	44 25

† times from passing Pontypool Road
* piloted by 2-4-0 No 587 (rebuilt 481 class)

start was leisurely, with speed not exceeding 59mph on the sharp descent to the river Usk crossing before Penpergwm; a first-class climb to Llanvihangel followed, with a minimum speed of 31mph. Although speed did not exceed 64mph at Pontrilas this had the makings of another 43-minute run until the train was stopped dead by signal at Red Hill Junction. In the next column a County, of which the recorder was not able to get the number and name, did well up to Llanvihangel summit, with a sustained minimum of 26mph. Speed then rose to 70mph before Pontrilas, but the train was repeatedly checked in the approach to Hereford, otherwise a time of 43 minutes from Pontypool Road would have been possible.

On the last of the five runs with a 310-ton train one of the Badmintons, by then rebuilt a second time with a standard No 2 boiler and superheated, was given a pilot. This was one of the rebuilt 481 class 2-4-0s which were the standard locomotives used from the Bristol end when the West to North service via the Severn Tunnel was inaugurated in 1888. As rebuilt they had 17in × 24in cylinders, and 150lb/sq in boiler pressure. The coupled wheels were 6ft 0in diameter. On this particular run the going was not particularly energetic. The start was

North to West express, climbing from Shrewsbury to Church Stretton, hauled by 2-4-0 No 440 and a County of the 1911 batch. (Locomotive Publishing Co)

leisurely, and speed fell to 26½mph on the Llanvihangel ascent. After that the two locomotives ran very gently down to Hereford to arrive just inside schedule time.

Continuing north from Hereford, there are included journeys already noticed, with the anonymous County and Flower No 4119 *Wynnstay*, together with two superb runs with Counties. Also, in view of the reputed inspiration behind the first introduction of these latter locomotives, I could not resist adding a run on the one-time 2.25am night mail from Hereford, worked by a Webb compound. The anonymous County with a light load and an easy schedule made an undistinguished run, and then comes the Webb 4-cylinder compound *Hindustan*, though at the time of the run modified by the addition of a separate Joy valve gear for the low-pressure cylinders. This alteration, made by George Whale, made a world of difference to the Alfred the Great class; even so the performance on this run, with a load of no more than 225 tons, was nothing very special. The 65-minute schedule of this train was kept only by a fast run downhill from Church Stretton, after 2½ minutes had been lost on the uphill sections. I should interpose here that for the first 28 miles out of Hereford the rise is gradual and continuous. Then after a fairly hard 30 to 35 minutes of running there comes the main pull up to Church Stretton, on gradients

GWR HEREFORD-SHREWSBURY

Run No:		1	2	3	4	5
Locomotive No:		38XX	1972*	4119	3834	3832
Locomotive Name:		–	Hindustan	Wynnstay	County of Somerset	County of Wilts
Load, tons, full		190	225	280	330	410
Distance Miles		Actual min sec	Actual min sec	Actual min sec	Actual min sec	Actual min sec
0.0	HEREFORD	0 00	0 00	0 00	0 00	0 00
7.5	Dinmore	10 00	11 30	12 15	10 29	11 25
12.6	Leominster	16 20	17 10	17 50	16 00	16 43
18.9	Woofterton	23 15	24 10	24 00	22 44	23 00
23.5	Ludlow	28 45	29 48	28 35	27 48	27 05
28.1	Onibury	34 00	35 03	33 35	33 22	32 49
31.1	Craven Arms	38 20	39 10	37 10	36 56	36 26
35.6	Marsh Brook	44 20	45 46	43 12	42 28	–
38.2	Church Stretton	48 00	50 27	47 30	46 00	47 18
44.6	Dorrington	54 40	56 20	54 03	51 58	53 10
–		–	–	sigs	–	sigs
51.0	SHREWSBURY	64 45	64 25	64 05	61 37	63 30

* LNWR 4-cylinder compound 4-4-0

averaging 1 in 197 between mileposts 22 and 13¾ (from Shrewsbury). Included in this latter stretch are five miles continuous at 1 in 103-112 from Craven Arms. The LNWR locomotive *Hindustan* took 35 minutes 3 seconds to pass Onibury, 28.1 miles, and then averaged 39.4mph up to Church Stretton.

On the third run *Wynnstay*, with its load reduced to 280 tons, and having shed its 2-4-0 pilot, made a slower start out of Hereford than the Webb compound, but then got going in great style, gaining 3½ minutes on the latter between Leominster and Church Stretton. Its uphill average of 43.6mph from Onibury was excellent, with a minimum speed of 33mph on the final 1 in 103. On the fourth run *County of Somerset*, with a 330-ton train, made a grand start out of Hereford, passing Dinmore in much the fastest time of the series; after that the locomotive was eased considerably until it was only just ahead of *Wynnstay* on passing Onibury. Then came a massive opening-out, for the 10.1 miles from there to Church Stretton took no more than 12 minutes 38 seconds an average of 47.9mph, and over the last 2.6 miles up from Marsh Brook the average speed was still as high as 44.2mph. No finer example of the potential of the County class than this can be quoted.

As if that were not good enough, there is lastly the fifth run, with a tremendous wartime load, when evidently one of the 4-6-0s was not available. While not getting away from Hereford so vigorously as on the previous run the driver and fireman of *County of Wilts* sustained the pressure continuously from Dinmore, with the result that on passing Ludlow the most heavily-loaded locomotive of all five was ahead of all competitors. The 16 miles from Dinmore to Ludlow took only 15 minutes 40 seconds and the average speed of 61.4mph with 410 tons was in some contrast to the 52.5mph of *Hindustan*, or the 58.7mph of *Wynnstay* with 280 tons. Then from Onibury the 10.1 miles up to Church Stretton were climbed in 14 minutes 29 seconds, 41.8mph average. The minimum speed above Marsh Brook was 34mph and with a maximum of 69mph downhill near Dorrington, the finishing time into Shrewsbury would have been about 61½ minutes but for the final signal check. This was a superb run, and once again gives the lie to those who suggest that the Counties were the least successful of all Churchward's standard designs.

With the end of the war and the emergence of working conditions that he found irksome after the degree of autonomy he had previously enjoyed, Churchward felt that his work was done, and at the end of 1921 he retired. Before that, however, the two-hour Birmingham service from Paddington had been restored, and although by that time 4-6-0 locomotives were generally used, the saga of the Counties on these trains was not quite ended—once to my own surprise and disappointment. In the early summer of 1921 the opportunity came to take some lineside photographs at Acocks Green and when one of the London trains came dashing along, to my disappointment (hoping for a Star) it was hauled by a County. Subsequently Cecil J. Allen clocked an excellent run on the sharply-timed 2.55pm up with *County of Bedford*. This,

No 3821 *County of Bedford*, in plain green. *(Real Photographs Ltd)*

GWR 2.55 p.m. BIRMINGHAM-PADDINGTON
Load: 294 tons tare, 315 tons full
Locomotive: No 3821 *County of Bedford*

Distance Miles		Schedule min.	Actual min sec	Speeds mph
0.0	BIRMINGHAM (SNOW HILL)	0	0 00	–
3.2	Tyseley		5 20	–
10.4	Knowle		12 35	67
12.9	Lapworth		14 35	76 ½
17.1	Hatton	18	18 15	–
21.3	Warwick		21 35	79
23.3	LEAMINGTON	26	23 55	–
6.1	Southam Road		10 20	45 ½
–			sigs.	–
11.1	Fenny Compton		17 10	–
16.2	Cropredy		23 10	67
19.8	BANBURY	24	27 10	–
5.1	*Aynho Junc*	6	7 55	60
10.3	Ardley		13 25	50
14.1	Bicester		16 45	82 ½ (max
20.1	Brill		21 15	62 ½
23.3	*Ashendon Junc*	23	24 25	(slack)
27.4	Haddenham		28 20	62 ½
32.8	PRINCES RISBOROUGH	33	33 55	53
36.0	Saunderton		37 45	46 ½
41.0	HIGH WYCOMBE	42	43 10	71 ½ /35*
45.8	Beaconsfield		48 55	56 ½ /52 ½
52.7	Denham		55 05	79
57.2	Northolt Junc	58	58 45	72 ½
59.7	Greenford	60	60 45	76 ½
62.9	Park Royal		63 20	–
–			sigs	–
64.2	*Old Oak West Junc*	65	65 35	–
–			sigs	–
67.5	PADDINGTON	70	73 45	–

* Speed restriction

as in pre-war years, was an Old Oak turn, but the Star that had worked down from Paddington on the 9.10am express had failed at Wolverhampton and the County was provided at short notice. The result was another superb run, set out in full detail in the accompanying table.

The start out of Birmingham was barely distinguishable from that of a Star, with speed increasing on the gradual rise to 56½mph by Solihull, to 66mph on the level to Knowle, and then tearing away to 76½mph at Lapworth troughs, and 79mph down Hatton bank. Then restarting from Leamington speed was sustained at 43½mph up Fosse Road bank, though a signal check caused a loss of three minutes to Banbury. Grand work followed with this 315-ton train, keeping very closely to the exacting point-to-point times required on this train. One can turn back in some curiosity to the runs made in the early years of this service, and referred to in the previous chapter, and compare them with this stalwart effort, which was not relaxed for one moment from start to finish. I do not think that, even without the signal check, exact time could have been kept from Leamington to Banbury, but against schedule times of 26, 24 and 70 minutes the net times were 24, 25 and 70 minutes. I wonder if it was in honorable memory of this run that Meccano Ltd. chose the name of *County of Bedford* for its '0' gauge model in the Hornby series?

It was in February 1923 that the rebuilding of the Armstrong class 4-4-0s was completed. In April 1915 Churchward had completely rebuilt No 16 *Brunel*, renumbering it 4169, replacing the original 7ft 1½in coupled wheels with the standard 6ft 8½in and substituting piston for the original slide valves. The locomotive had previously been superheated with the standard No 2 taper boiler, and it was then completely assimilated to the Flower class. No 14 *Charles Saunders* was similarly treated in May 1917, but the other two remained as 7-footers. Both had been superheated in 1911, but while No 7 *Armstrong* had the long-coned taper boiler, No No 8 *Gooch* had since superheating two subsequent changes of boiler, and at the end of

1922 had one of the short-coned type. These two locomotives were rebuilt to conform with the others in 1923 and were renumbered 4171 and 4172. The order of this final numbering referred to the order of conversion rather than the original numerical sequence below.

Reference has been made earlier to the very thorough programme of superheating applied to all the domeless boilered classes covered by this book, but the collateral process of fitting them with piston valves was spread over a much longer period. At the time of Churchward's retirement in December 1921 a total of 41 Bulldogs remained with the original slide valves, and of these 12 were never converted to piston valves. A similar situation prevailed in the case of the Atbaras, Cities and Flowers. Except for the unfortunate *Mafeking*, which was scrapped in 1911 after the destructive accident at Henley-in-Arden, the whole stud of inside-cylinder 4-4-0s passed intact into the Collett era. Furthermore, as described in detail in Chapter 6, work was pressed ahead with the super-heating of the Dukes.

'ARMSTRONG' CLASS 4-4-0s

Date fitted 6ft 8½in wheels and piston valves	Original Number	Name	New Number
April 1915	16	*Brunel*	4169
May 1917	14	*Charles Saunders*	4170
February 1923	7	*Armstrong*	4171
February 1923	8	*Gooch*	4172

Paddington-Ilfracombe express on Mortehoe bank (SR line) hauled by a Bulldog and banked by an ex-LSWR M7 0-4-4T. *(A. Halls)*

Down Weymouth express near Aldermaston, with No 3829 *County of Merioneth. (L & GRP)*

Collett's early construction work was concerned almost entirely with the multiplication of Churchward's standard classes, and with new and enlarged 4-cylinder 4-6-0s, but by the end of 1925 the whole motive power situation on the GWR was changing. No fewer than 322 of the standard 2-6-0s were at work, while the addition of 12 more Stars (Abbey series) and 20 Castles released some of the Saint class for use on routes hitherto having nothing larger than 4-4-0s. Only the Bristol-Birmingham line remained an exclusive 4-4-0 preserve, because of the restriction imposed by the LMS over the section between Standish Junction and Yate. There was another factor looming up. In 1925 No 2925 *Saint Martin* had been rebuilt with 6ft 0in coupled wheels, instead of the original 6ft 8½in, and the success of this prototype as a fast mixed-traffic locomotive presaged the introduction of the celebrated Hall class in 1928. This

Birkenhead-Bournemouth express near Pangbourne, hauled by a Bulldog class 4-4-0. *(E. Little)*

was indeed the death-knell of the 6ft 8½in inside-cylinder 4-4-0s, and withdrawal had begun early in 1927. The first to go was Atbara No 4125 *Khartoum* in April of that year, an event that I shall always remember from an incident in the offices of the Locomotive Publishing Company shortly afterwards. On free Saturdays I used occasionally to go to Amen Corner to buy photographs from that famous collection and on that particular morning a senior man, whose name I never knew, spoke with tears in his eyes about the demise of *Khartoum*. 'Before long', he exclaimed, 'there will not be a four-coupled engine left in the country.' An exaggeration certainly, but for the GWR 6ft 8½in 4-4-0s the writing was definitely on the wall.

The withdrawals proceeded steadily over the ensuing years, and in cold print may be statistically analysed thus:

LOCOMOTIVES WITHDRAWN

Year	Armstrong	Badminton	Atbara	Flower	City	Total
1927	–	6	10	6	1	23
1928	2	3	7	2	4	18
1929	1	4	6	8	12	31
1930	1	4	4	3	1	13
1931	–	3	2	1	2	8
Total	4	20	29	20	20	93

While the complete list of the dates of withdrawal are given in the case histories at the end of this book, a few notes on famous individual locomotives are not inappropriate at this stage. Of the Badmintons, No 4105 *Earl Cawdor* which in its early life went through so many vicissitudes of boiler changes was one of those to go in 1927, while another celebrated locomotive of this series, *Waterford*, went even earlier, in July of that year. *Atbara*, used for so many special trains around the turn of the century went in September 1929, while No 4121 *Baden Powell*, which at different times had three special names substituted for the true one, was withdrawn in December 1928. No 4146 *Sydney*, as No 3410 the prototype of the beautiful Bassett-Lowke model, was one of the first to go, in October 1927. The last Atbara to survive was No 4148 *Singapore*, until May 1931. The one Flower to survive until 1931 was the locomotive of the official photograph, No 4150, originally No 4102 *Begonia*.

The principal slaughter of the Cities took place in 1929, when 12 out of the 20 went. The first to go in October 1927 was *City of Winchester*, which still retained slide valves at the time of its withdrawal. No 3708 *Killarney*, which I well remember working on the Chester road in 1926, was withdrawn in 1929, while the very last was No 3712 *City of Bristol*, in May 1931. The ever-famous No 3717 *City of Truro*

No 3803 *County Cork* with short safety-valve cover. *(Real Photographs Co Ltd)*

had been taken out of traffic in March 1931 and was at once presented to the York Railway Museum. In its issue of May 1931 *The Railway Magazine* waxed lyrical in its editorial comment:

Not yet is the romance of the railway quite dead. But few of those who follow the fortunes of the steam locomotive, with both interest and affection, can have failed to be stirred, to some degree at least, by the news that the famous Great Western locomotive *City of Truro* is to find a permanent resting-place in the York Railway Museum. To a wider public also the event is not without its significance. It is, indeed, a recognition of the fact that high speed on the railway is not the useless and unnecessary extravagance that it is sometimes represented to be. For *City of Truro* is responsible for having achieved the highest railway speed record ever authenticated by a competent observer in this country. At the time it was recorded—May 9, 1904—this was in all probability, indeed, the highest speed which up till that time had been reached by

No 3717 *City of Truro* as first installed in the old Railway Museum at York. *(O. S. Nock)*

any mechanically-propelled vehicle. It is thus of all the more importance that, when new records of fast travel are being achieved constantly by land, sea and air, steps have been taken to preserve the locomotive which lays claim to the maximum speed yet attained on British metals, even though the occasion is now past by more than a quarter of a century.

The preservation of *City of Truro* certainly started something. It spurred other enthusiasts to campaign for the preservation of other famous locomotives, and within a year LNWR 2-4-0 No 790 *Hardwicke* and Caledonian 4-2-2 No 123 were saved from the scrap heap. But *City of Truro* started something else less palatable, nothing less than a vigorous attempt to discredit the record maximum speed claimed by Charles Rous-Marten, and accepted without question for 27 years. In every age, and in every walk of life there have been men who have delighted in attempting to dethrone idols, or to debunk cherished beliefs, and the campaign waged in *The Railway Magazine* in 1934 was a classic example. I found the arguments put forward confusing and unconvincing, but at the time I was in no position to intervene personally; I was

disappointed that some of those whose word then carried much weight were inclined to shrug their shoulders and accept that the record was discredited.

The matter came before me in some urgency in 1953, when I was commissioned to write a book *Fifty Years of Western Express Running*, the publication of which was to synchronise with the 50th anniversary of the Ocean Mails contest with the London & South Western Railway. Clearly the confused aspersions cast on the

No 3702 *Halifax* on Oxford-Paddington express near Twyford. *(M. W. Earley)*

veracity of Rous-Marten's figures could not be left as they had lain since 1934. Some 20 years later, however, with much first-hand experience of locomotive running, and my professional engineering work, particularly in the operation

Up Oxford and Worcester express on the slow line east of Twyford, with No 3716 *City of London*. *(H. Gordon Tidey)*

of railway brakes, as a background, I was in a much stronger position to analyse, and re-assess the data published by Rous-Marten. The detailed argument was given in my book of 1954, and repeated in my book *Speed Records on Britain's Railways*, in 1971. As I wrote then, I feel that a speed of *at least* 100mph may be accepted on behalf of *City of Truro* and its crew.

In 1930, when at last the LMS was prepared to accept 4-6-0 locomotives over the Yate-Standish line, withdrawal of the Counties began. Five out of the six condemned were of the first batch of 1904, together with No 3807 *County Kilkenny*, but in 1931 no fewer than 25 of them were scrapped. While one could feel justifiably sad at the passing of so many old and trusted friends, there was an added significance in the vigour of proceedings at Swindon in that for the first time Saint class 4-6-0s were among those withdrawn, three of them in 1931. Of the nine remaining Counties, four went in 1932 and the last five in 1933, No 3834 *County of Somerset* being the very last, in November of that year.

When the new Hall class 4-6-0s were put on to the Wolverhampton-Penzance express, my friends A. V. Goodyear and J. C. Keyte logged a number of interesting performances over the North Warwickshire line, especially noticing the ascent of the Henley bank. As sometimes happens on the inception of a new class, there

No 3827 *County of Gloucester* in plain green. *(Real Photographs Co Ltd)*

came a day when one of them was not available for this important turn and No 3812 *County of Cardigan* was used instead. The result was another run in near-heroic mould, as shown by the accompanying log. It began, however, with near-ignominy. The station at Stratford-on-Avon

GWR STRATFORD-ON-AVON - BIRMINGHAM
Load: 246 tons tare, 255 tons full
Locomotive: No 3812 *County of Cardigan*

Distance Miles		Actual min sec	Average speeds mph
0.0	Stratford-on-Avon	0 00	—
2.6	Wilmcote	4 55	31.7
5.5	*Milepost 16*	7 47	60.8
8.0	Henley-in-Arden	10 16	60.2
11.0	Danzey	13 22	58.1
12.8	Wood End	15 20	54.9
14.8	Earlswood Lakes	17 30	55.3
17.6	Shirley	20 07	64.4
20.1	Hall Green	22 10	73.0
21.7	Tyseley	23 46	60.0
—		sigs	—
25.0	Birmingham (Snow Hill)	29 55	—

Speeds:	*Actual mph*	
	Milepost 16	68
	Wood End	54
	Earlswood	55½
	Hall Green	75

Equivalent drawbar horsepower at Wood End: 925

has a gradient of 1 in 227 from the platform end, and with trains of any weight it was customary to provide rear-end banking assistance just out of the platform. In the contrary way of things no banker was available on this occasion and *County of Cardigan* stalled at its first attempt to

No 3812 *County of Cardigan*, with non-gartered crest on tender, and short safety-valve cover. *(Real Photographs Co Ltd)*

get away. But the driver did not mince matters on his second attempt, and seeing the initial time of 4 minutes 55 seconds to Wilmcote one would hardly suspect that the distance of 2.6 miles included 1½ miles up at 1 in 75! Then speed rose to 68mph after Bearley, and the train was taken up the entire 7½ miles of 1 in 150 at a sustained minimum speed of 54mph, increasing to 55½mph on the final 1 in 181 to Earlswood Lakes. This big effort involved a continued equivalent drawbar horsepower of 925, and was a fitting counterpart to the runs of *County of Wilts* on the Hereford-Shrewsbury line, and *County of Bedford* on the 2.55pm from Birmingham to Paddington.

Neither must I forget the occasion when one of them worked the Cheltenham Flyer. Some 30 years ago, in the Journal of the Stephenson Locomotive Society, Mr V. R. Webster wrote:

In the early 1920's No 3820 *County of Worcester* stood as down pilot at Reading seemingly for years. When the Cheltenham Flyer was first put on in 1924 it was worked every day by 2915 *Saint Batholomew* which at that time travelled to Swindon with a down milk empties train, returning with the 3.45pm up 'Flyer' in 75 minutes. One day 2915 developed a fault at Reading on the down journey and *County of Worcester* was hastily requisitioned to take the milk train on to

Swindon. There was wild speculation alike among enthusiasts and station staff, and word got around that *County of Worcester* was to perform on the 'Flyer' that afternoon. By 4.20 there was an appreciable crowd of spectators. The up 'Limited' was safely through and out of the way punctually at 4.8 and many watches were being consulted as the hour for the 'Flyer's' passage approached. Sure enough, at about 4.20 she was signalled, and right on time 3820 came pounding through the station, lurching over the junctions as only Counties could lurch and giving a seemingly extra long whistle, which was held from the engine sheds right through the station. It was wildly cheered by a large group of enthusiasts who all prophesied that 'the thing couldn't run fast' and to the obvious interest of the Reading crew of the new down pilot—now a Mogul.

I should add that then the Cheltenham Flyer was allowed 75 minutes for the 77.3 mile non-stop run from Swindon to Paddington, and with this average speed of 61.8mph was the fastest train in the British Isles. The load was usually one of eight coaches, mixed 60ft 'concertina' and clerestory stock, and weighing about 225 tons full. The booked time through Reading was 4.25pm so that if indeed it passed soon after 4.20pm the train would have been several minutes ahead of time. Bravo *County of Worcester*!

Withdrawal of the Bulldogs, but on no more than a limited scale, was already under way by the early 1930s. The first to go was No 3320 *Avalon* in August 1929, but that was the only one in that year, while only two more followed in 1930. Both these latter were locomotives deserving more than a passing reference. No 3365 *Charles Grey Mott* withdrawn in January 1930, was the victim of a mistake in Volume 1 of this book, where on page 54 I stated that it had been renamed *Lord Mildmay of Flete*. This was because of mixing up the original and the later numbers of these locomotives. The original number of 3365 was 3417, and it was the Bulldog that latterly bore the number 3417, originally 3707 *Francis Mildmay* that in 1923 was renamed *Lord Mildmay of Flete*. The second withdrawn in 1930 was No 3334 *Tavy*, which in 1904 made British railway history in being fitted with a mechanical stoker. This was an interesting example of Churchward's willingness to try out any device that gave promise of improved working. The stoker was later transferred to Atbara 4-4-0 No 4127 *Ladysmith*. Another six Bulldogs were withdrawn in 1931,

No 3743 *Seagull*, prior to renumbering as 3453 on up West of England express. *(Locomotive Publishing Co)*

followed by seven in 1932, but the process was relatively slow, and will be referred to in more detail in the final chapter of this book.

In the meantime the rest of the class remained in very active service. I had a run with one of them on the 6.50pm from Chester to Wrexham in April 1936. The locomotive was No 3373, which when built in May 1903 as No 3425 carried the name *Sir W. H. Wills*. In January 1906 it was desired to put the gentleman's name in full, but *Sir William Henry Wills* was too long for the nameplates, and so from that time onward the locomotive was titled *Sir William Henry*. Name or not, it gave me a good run, with a gross load of 190 tons. We ran gently down to Saltney Junction, taking 4 minutes 9 seconds for that first 1.8 miles, and then picked up smartly on the undulating and slightly rising length to Rossett, touching 57mph. Then came Gresford bank, with four miles continuously at 1 in 82½. Up this we went splendidly, not falling below 33½mph until slackened to 10mph for a pitfall restriction near Wheatsheaf Junction. To cover this difficult 12.1 miles from Chester to Wrexham in 18¾ minutes was good work.

Later that same year No 3342 *Bonaventura*, assisted a Castle on a smart run from Plymouth to Newton Abbot, with a gross load of 365 tons. Because of a permanent way restriction at Tavistock Junction, they had not attained more than 48mph at the foot of Hemerdon bank, but did not fall below 22mph at the top. Some unusually brisk running was made downhill

from Wrangaton, touching 68mph in the descent of Rattery bank. Totnes was passed at exactly 60mph and the 4.8 miles up to Dainton summit took only 5 minutes 35 seconds with a minimum of 30½mph, and despite the initial check Newton Abbot, 31.8 miles, was reached in 42 minutes 5 seconds. It would have seemed that the Bulldog and its crew were the main source of inspiration, because afterwards the work of the Castle on its own was not enterprising. On another occasion, with the up Cornish Riviera Express, a King took assistance from Plymouth with a tare load of 370 tons. I know that 360 tons was the official maximum load over the South

South Wales-Portsmouth express emerging from the Severn Tunnel, hauled by No 3407 *Madras. (G. H. Soole)*

Devon line, but on this occasion, with two minutes spent in putting off the pilot at Hemerdon the time to passing Wrangaton was two minutes longer than that of another run, with only 5 tons less load, on which no assistance had been taken. This of course was no reflection on the pilot locomotive No 3401 *Vancouver,* which helped the King to reach Hemerdon in 12½ minutes start to stop from Plymouth North Road.

CHAPTER SIX

DUKES AND DUKEDOGS

In the grouping of 1923 the Cambrian Railways became part of the Great Western, and the headquarters of the former company at Oswestry became a divisional outpost of Swindon so far as locomotives were concerned, It had never been a prosperous concern, and this was reflected in the age and relatively small power of the locomotive stock. The very latest passenger locomotives of the 4-4-0 type, dated back to 1904 and at the time of grouping only four of them remained. One had been completely destroyed in the terrible head-on collision near Abermule in 1921. Although these locomotives worked the heavier trains the mainstay of the passenger service were the 21

Down Oxford express passing Old Oak Common: Duke class 4-4-0 No 3276 *St. Agnes* with a heavy load. *(F. E. Mackay)*

4-4-0s of Aston's design dating back to 1893. But there was another difficulty that also arose through lack of finance, and that was the light nature of the track and underline bridge structures. The civil engineer's department of the GWR, after Grouping, classified the Cambrian main line and the coast section from Dovey Junction to Barmouth and Portmadoc as yellow routes, which meant that not even the Bulldogs could be run over them. The only existing Great Western locomotives acceptable were the Dukes, the surviving 2-4-0s, the Dean goods 0-6-0s, and the small-wheel 3521 class 4-4-0s. Something had to be done about it, and quickly; this situation, to the delight of GWR enthusiasts, prolonged for many years the life of the Dukes.

The Cambrian locomotives of the 94 class

Train from Didcot approaching Southampton hauled by Duke class 4-4-0 No 3261 *St. Germans. (D. S. M. Barrie)*

were actually of more recent origin than the Dukes, and on the line itself they were considered ideal for the job; they had been designed specially by Herbert Jones and built by Robert Stephenson & Co. It is interesting to compare their leading dimensions with those of the Dukes, thus:

Railway Class	Cambrian 94	GWR Duke
Cylinders, dia, in	18½	18
Cylinders, stroke, in	26	26
Coupled wheel dia	6ft 0in	5ft 8in
Heating surfaces sq ft — tubes	1166	1285.58
firebox	117	112.6
Grate area sq ft	20.5	19.0
Boiler pressure lb/sq in	170	160
Nominal tractive effort (85% boiler pressure) lb	17,900	16,848
Total weight, locomotive only, tons	45.2	46
Adhesion weight, tons	29.65	28.5

The above dimensions relate to the Dukes as built and make a direct comparison to the Cambrian locomotives when new in 1904. At the time of the grouping most of the Dukes had the standard type Belpaire firebox boilers, which carried a pressure of 180lb/sq in. The adhesion weight was 29.1 tons, with a maximum axle load of 14.6 tons, as compared to the 15.3 tons of the Cambrian engines. With 180lb/sq in pressure the nominal tractive effort was 18,970lb. The

Duke was thus very acceptable for the Cambrian line.

At the time of grouping 15 of the Dukes had been superheated, but there was no undue haste shown in thus modernising the remainder to equip them for their new-found main line task. The transfer to new duties was fairly gradual, and by 1926 although a number of them had been seen at various times on the Cambrian line, there were only about 10 regularly allocated there, five at Oswestry, two more at Shrewsbury, and working across to Welshpool, and a few at Aberystwyth. At one time there were four at Tyseley, but this latter allocation was typical of the way they became spread around the system. Apart from odd jobs, which the few stationed at depots like Reading, Westbury, Newton Abbot and Laira performed, there became three main spheres of activity for the class. There was the Didcot, Newbury & Southampton line, for which there were usually six Dukes stationed at Didcot, while in addition to the Cambrian, there was the former Midland & South Western Junction Railway. This latter line, contrary to what its name might suggest, was not a joint line but a wholly-independent concern until the grouping of 1923. Then, although its traffic affiliations were almost entirely with the Midland at one end and with the London & South Western at the other, on a territorial basis it lay entirely within the Great Western fold and it duly became one of the so-called subsidiary companies of the enlarged GWR, to the chagrin of most of its staff.

Although encompassed by great and famous railways at all its exchange points, there had grown up a very proud and independent tradition among the men who worked on the MSWJR, though how it got its homely nickname I have no idea. There were two variations of this, in my hearing. At the Cheltenham end it was 'Chidley Dyke', but in Swindon, among Great Western men it was usually just 'Tiddley'. A draughtsman who worked for me many years ago came from a large Swindon family all of whom were footplate men. At first I assumed that they were Great Western; but oh dear no! They were 'Midland', and the sense of pride and superiority with which the name was uttered rather suggested that Brunel's route which ran beneath them at Rushey Platt was a small local concern! One can then imagine how the 'Chidley' men felt when the GWR took them over and began rebuilding their locomotives with taper boilers and other specialities from the 'other' part of Swindon. The situation was not so pressing as on the Cambrian, because the MSWJR locomotive stock was in good shape and the line was not beset by the gradient difficulties, nor the prospects of an increasing summer traffic that was inclined to embarrass the motive power department of the Cambrian. By the time the MSWJR was absorbed by the Great Western the ambitious provision of through carriages between Southampton and various northern destinations reached over the Midland Railway had dwindled to one, and the purely MSWJR service between Southampton and Cheltenham did not present a very severe task for the locomotives. Nevertheless the complete run, exercising running powers over the LSWR section of the Southern Railway, from Andover via Romsey and Redbridge, involved a continuous run of 97 miles.

The MSWJR had a locomotive shed of its own at Cheltenham, but when the Dukes began to take over they worked from Gloucester, and by 1926 six had been seen on these duties. These were Nos 3260 *Mount Edgcumbe*, 3261 *St. Germans*, 3263 *St. Michael*, 3269 *Dartmoor*, 3284 *Isle of Jersey*, and 3290 *Severn*. No 3261

was one of those that had nameplates removed in the early 1930s because the Traffic Department feared that they might be mistaken for train destinations, though I can hardly imagine that the sight of No 3261 would give the country folk using the homely 'Chidley Dyke' trains any ideas that they were about to be whisked off to Cornwall! Names apart, the Dukes were ideal for the line, and the way in which they were accepted by the local men was another tribute to the excellence of their design and to the manner in which they had been maintained over the years.

Their assignment to the Cambrian was a much more severe test of capacity. The Dukes were designed for stiff hill-climbing, and they had had plenty of practice in South Devon and Cornwall. Down in the West Country, though, there was nothing like the Talerddig bank, the dominant feature of the entire Cambrian main line between Whitchurch and Aberystwyth. Furthermore, the whole business of running trains was complicated not only by the existence of single line over the entire 95½ miles of route between Whitchurch and Aberystwyth save for two short sections—Oswestry to Llanymynech and Buttington to Forden—but that the passing loops, which numbered 24 in all, involved drastic slowings for hand exchange of the single-line tokens. The Cambrian could not afford to install the more sophisticated systems of token exchange to permit of running at 50 to 55mph through the loops. Even on the express trains' runs there was a continuous succession of slows and subsequent vigorous accelerations. Gradient-wise, although there are some sharp intermediate undulations, the line is not difficult in the 52 miles from Whitchurch to Moat Lane Junction, but then there comes the climb to Talerddig, not generally severe from the eastern side, but eight miles of hard going nevertheless, with pitches at 1 in 71 and 1 in 80. The climb from the western side, however, can be a killer. Three miles out of Machynlleth comes the first, or 'easy' stretch with 6 miles averaging about 1 in 100. Then comes nearly a mile at 1 in 60 up to Llanbrynmair, a level 'breather' through the loop, and then 3¼ miles at 1 in 52-56 up to the summit.

Cambrian enthusiasts, after the amalgamation, claimed bitterly that although the 94 class 4-4-0s were classified with the Bulldogs for load haulage, and were thus expected to haul a few more tons unassisted than the Dukes, the GWR so strictly regulated the individual locomotive loads that the ex-Cambrian locomotives were not allowed to tackle unassisted the tonnages they were reputed to take in pre-Grouping days. This was probably a piece of local partisanship, because by the table on page 71 the nominal tractive effort of the 94 class was less than that of the Dukes in the form they were when put on to the Cambrian line. The load ratings established for the Dukes was 238 tons tare as a general line maximum, and 182 tons between Machynlleth and Talerddig eastbound. For most of the way round the coastal section from Machynlleth to Aberystwyth the line is dead level with two short gables having 1 in 75 gradients in the last 7 miles.

As to personalia of the locomotives first transferred to the Cambrian section, the following allocations were noted up to 1926, though there was much interchange between sheds as individual locomotives were called into Swindon for overhaul, and subsequently allocated elsewhere. In 1926 Shrewsbury had Nos 3257 *King Arthur* and 3270 *Earl of Devon* for working through Aberystwyth sections of London trains to Welshpool and beyond; Oswestry had Nos 3252 *Duke of Cornwall*, 3259 *Merlin*, 3264 *Trevithick*, 3280 *Tregenna* and 3291 *Thames*. Of the above seven, No 3257 had its name removed in 1927 for fear of confusion with the new King class 4-6-0s, and more justifiably No 3280 was similarly robbed when one of the new Castles was named *Tregenna Castle*. For a time Nos 3271 *Eddystone* and 3276 *St. Agnes* were stationed at Aberystwyth. At about the same time the Didcot contingent, for working over the line to Southampton via Newbury included Nos 3254 *Cornubia*, 3274 *Newquay* and 3282. The last-mentioned had originally been *Chepstow Castle*, but had been nameless since the new 4-6-0 of 1923 took that name.

By the end of 1929 another 13 of the Dukes had been superheated, but it is interesting to find that no specific allocation of superheater locomotives was made for the severe duties of the Cambrian line, and that of those specifically noted in the previous paragraph two, *Eddystone* and *Merlin*, remained non-superheated until their final withdrawal in 1936 and 1938 respectively; *Trevithick* was not superheated until 1944, but still five years before it was withdrawn. In Cambrian days, before loads at holiday seasons became so heavy, it had been the practice to provide rear-end banking assistance to Talerddig, and allow the train engines to struggle over the line elsewhere; with plenty of Dukes available it became Great Western practice to run a pair of them throughout when loads exceeded 238 tons tare. Two of them together were expected to take 360 tons up the Talerddig bank and this covered almost all requirements. In 1927 five additional members of the class were reported as regularly working on the Cambrian line, namely Nos 3256 *Guinevere*, 3273 *Mounts Bay*, 3277 *Isle of Tresco*, 3287 *Mercury* and 3288 *Mendip*, though like some other working these should be taken as probably no more than transitory, and not permanent. They are however enough to show the movement of the class, and the importance placed upon it in the general motive power strategy of the GWR, when wholesale scrapping of the 6ft 8in 4-4-0s was proceeding towards its conclusion.

By the mid-1930s the Dukes were ageing. There is a limit to the extent that old frames can be patched, and the frame is inevitably the foundation on which the locomotive is based. The pattern for the immediate future had been shown in December 1929 when No 3265 *Tre Pol*

No 3200, in the brief period when named *Earl of Mount Edgcumbe*. (British Railways)

and Pen was withdrawn. A month later the second of the Bulldogs was withdrawn, No 3365 *Charles Grey Mott*. I am never likely to forget that one from the sheer weight of correspondence, some distinctly abrasive, that descended on me after I had inadvertently confused it under its original number of 3417 with another Bulldog which became 3417 after the 1912 renumbering. But to revert to the year 1930, the frames of No 3365 were apparently in good condition, and a most curious rebuilding took place in which the cylinders and motion from No 3265 and a spare Duke boiler were fitted to make what was at first noted as no more than a straight-framed rebuild of a Duke. The original number and name *Tre Pol and Pen* were retained. For some reason that I have never been able to discover the bogie wheels were 3ft 2in as on the 4-6-0 express passenger locomotives with 6ft 8½in coupled wheels. It was probably necessary to provide clearance in the fitting of the Duke cylinders and motion to the Bulldog frames. As thus rebuilt *Tre Pol and Pen* had the following weight distribution, compared to those of the Dukes with Belpaire fire box boilers, and with the Bulldogs:

		Coupled Wheels	
Class	Bogie	Leading	Trailing
	ton cwt	ton cwt	ton cwt
Duke	18 4	14 12	14 10
Bulldog	17 8	17 12	16 16
Tre Pol and Pen	18 12	15 8	15 0

The rebuilding with straight frames therefore did not preclude the use of *Tre Pol and Pen* on the Cambrian line.

The need to follow up this interesting rebuild did not arise for another five years, but by 1935 many of the Dukes were reaching a stage when it was becoming uneconomic to repair them, and because engineering limitations still precluded the use of larger locomotives on the Cambrian line the decision was taken to rebuild a number of Bulldogs with Duke class boilers. Between March 1936 and June 1938 a total of 20 Dukes was withdrawn, and replaced by a like number of Bulldogs rebuilt with Duke boilers. The first to be treated thus was No 3412 *John G. Griffiths*, which re-appeared as No 3201. Because it replaced the Duke No 3263 the original name of the latter, *St. Michael*, was at first perpetuated, and was carried for about a month. The rebuilt locomotive had the same general proportions as *Tre Pol and Pen*, but used the bogie previously standard to the 5ft 8in 4-4-0s, with 3ft 8in diameter wheels. These larger wheels did not apparently make any difference to the weight distribution, which according to the diagram was exactly the same as for *Tre Pol and Pen*. It had originally been proposed to perpetuate the Duke names, of which *St. Michael* was the first, but following the system of class nomenclature it was decided to give these rebuilds the names of Earls, all of living personalities connected in some way with the Great Western Railway. A selection of 20 was made to cover the first batch authorised

No 3209 *Earl of Radnor*, outside Swindon works. *(British Railways)*

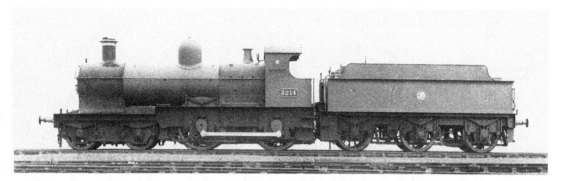

No 3214, which should have been *Earl Waldegrave*, but which never bore the name. *(British Railways)*

under Swindon Lot No 315, and programmed for 1936-38. The following names were chosen for Nos 3200-3219:

3200	*Earl of Mount Edgcumbe*
3201	*Earl of Dunraven*
3202	*Earl of Dudley*
3203	*Earl Cawdor*
3204	*Earl of Dartmouth*
3205	*Earl of Devon*
3206	*Earl of Plymouth*
3207	*Earl of St. Germans*
3208	*Earl Bathurst*
3209	*Earl of Radnor*
3210	*Earl Cairns*
3211	*Earl of Ducie*
3212	*Earl of Eldon*
3213	*Earl of Powis*
3214	*Earl Waldegrave*
3215	*Earl of Clancarty*
3216	*Earl St. Aldwyn*
3217	*Earl of Berkeley*
3218	*Earl of Birkenhead*
3219	*Earl of Shaftesbury*

Construction and naming as above had proceeded as far as No 3212, completed at Swindon in May 1937, and then suddenly, before any more were turned out, all the names were removed. They had all disappeared by 1 July 1937. The story goes that certain gentlemen objected to their names being carried on locomotives that were of a status much below the dignity and eminence they deserved, and that the locomotive department was ordered to remove the names forthwith. In about a month the withdrawn names began to appear on the 5043-5062 series of Castle class 4-6-0s, and the transposition of all 20 was completed by November 1937. The Earls, or more strictly the 32XX class of 4-4-0s, thereafter ran without names. Shorn of their original title of the Earl class some wag suggested that the measure of cross-breeding in which they had come into

existence should be recorded in a special title—'Dukedogs'—and that nickname has persisted to the point, almost, of official recognition.

The rejuvenated locomotives took the places of the Dukes. It had originally been intended to have 40 of them, but work on the second batch of 20 had progressed only so far as No 3227 by the outbreak of war in 1939, and only one more was converted, to leave Swindon in November 1939. Including *Tre Pol and Pen* this gave a total of 30, and at that time 10 Dukes remained. All these latter, of which scrapping did not begin until 1949, passed thus into British Railways ownership, and in view of their longevity it is worth while supplementing the case histories at the end of this book by a separate tabulation.

THE LAST TEN DUKES

Later number	Final BR number	Name	Date built	Date withdrawn
3254	9054	*Cornubia*	July 1985	June 1950
3264	9064	*Trevithick*	June 1896	Dec. 1949
3272	9072	*(Fowey)**	Jan. 1897	June 1949
3273	9073	*Mounts Bay*	Feb. 1897	Dec. 1949
3276	9076	*(St. Agnes)**	Mar. 1897	Nov. 1949
3283	9083	*Comet*	Mar. 1899	Dec. 1950
3284	9084	*Isle of Jersey*	April 1899	April 1951
3287	9087	*Mercury*	April 1899	July 1949
3289	9089	*(St. Austell)**	July 1899	July 1951
3291	9091	*Thames*	July 1899	Feb. 1949

* name removed

Thus *Cornubia* was the longest-lived, all but 55 years, and the unnamed 3289 was the last to survive.

At the end of 1939 the allocation of the 32XX class was 18 to the Cambrian line, distributed between Oswestry, Machynlleth and Aberystwyth, and the remainder distributed between Didcot, Gloucester, Shrewsbury, Swindon, Tyseley, and Wolverhampton (Stafford Road). The 32XX class carried on the good work done by the Dukes on the Cambrian line during the last years of peace; but during the war both that line and the Didcot, Newbury & Southampton were up-graded to the 'Blue' category, which meant that 43XX Moguls and the new Manor class 4-6-0s could work over them. This removed the principal *raison d'être* for both the 32XX class and the remaining Dukes, but it was not until after nationalisation that any withdrawals began. Then curiously enough it was the 32XX class that began to go first. The whole class had been renumbered 9000-9028 in the same order as previously in 1946, and it was Nos 9006, 9007 and 9019 that were withdrawn in 1948. Then there was a pause until 1954 when Nos 9001 and 9002 were scrapped.

In the summer of 1950 I had the pleasure of making some footplate journeys over the Cambrian line, and while I was then primarily interested in the working of the Manor class 4-6-0s, I was fortunate to get one run on a Dukedog, though with a load from Machynlleth that needed pilot assistance up to Talerddig. This was on the 12.30pm Saturdays-only express from Aberystwyth to Birmingham, calling only at Moat Lane, Newtown and Welshpool. I had

Dukedogs Nos 9025 and 9022 approaching Aberystwyth on a stopping train. *(E. D. Bruton)*

been staying at Barmouth overnight, and before leaving in the morning I saw come through that monumental Saturdays-only special from Pennychain, serving the holiday camp near Pwllheli, to Pontyridd. It ran down the coast through Barmouth, and from Dovey Junction followed the Cambrian main line to Moat Lane Junction, whence it took the Wye Valley line eventually reaching Merthyr, before its final spin down the Taff Vale. I saw it with 10 crowded coaches double-headed with two Dukedogs. They would have taken it no further than Moat Lane, because there it had to reverse direction. Studying its working times I often wondered if it ever managed to clock into Pontypridd exactly on the scheduled time (in the working book) of 4.33½pm!

When later that day my own train was wired from Aberystwyth as 221 tons, and therefore needing a bank engine up to Talerddig, I hoped that we might have had a second Dukedog coupled ahead, but we had instead a 45XX class 2-6-2 tank. In Cambrian days heavy trains were banked in rear, but in view of the speeds attained on the easier part of the climb the second locomotive was attached in front. The Dukedog No 9027 was excellent, riding well and steaming freely. It was fired with that precision and care that one saw everywhere on the old GWR, with the steel flap raised between each

Pwllheli to Paddington express climbing the Talerddig bank, in 1953, hauled by two Dukedogs Nos 9003 and 9000. (L. N. Owen)

shovelful, and pressure kept just up to sizzling point without at any time full blowing-off. Because of heavy traffic on this summer Saturday, and the presence of a stopping train ahead, we did not get a very good road at first, and we were stopped by signals at both Cemmes Road and Llanbrynmair. Between the stops our driver was using between 25 and 30 per cent cut-off, with the regulator about one-half open. So the 1 in 52 from Llanbrynmair had to be tacked from a standing start. With two locomotives and 235 tons gross between them this was not difficult. No 9027 was worked in 32 to 35 per cent cut-off, with regulator opened well out on to the second valve, and we could see and hear that the 2-6-2 tank leading was also going hard. Speed was held at 28 to 30mph on the 1 in 52.

The interesting part of the run with No 9027 began at Moat Lane, when we were down on to easier gradients and the line ahead was clear for us to make some speed. A smart run followed over the 4.6 miles to Newtown, undulating but almost level in the aggregate. The driver used 35 per cent cut-off in getting away, and then 25 per cent with a fairly wide regulator opening. Speed rose to 56mph before the stop, made in 7½ minutes from Moat Lane. The last 13.7 miles into Welshpool were booked in 25 minutes including three slowings for tablet exchange, one at that place of tragic memory, Abermule. The crossing places came in rapid succession, at 3.9, 7.5 and 9.5 miles from the start. It was in leaving Moat Lane that No 9027 misbehaved for the one and only time in the trip, priming slightly. We touched 52mph before the first tablet slack and 54½mph before the second. The approach to the third at Forden was hindered by a permanent way slack to 15mph, but on the last stretch into Welshpool, now on double-line, speed was worked briskly up to 65mph, the locomotive continuing to run very smoothly. The 14.8 miles from Newtown took 21½ minutes despite the check. The whole run had been made with ease and economy, and I was sorry that we were booked to change locomotives at Welshpool, getting in exchange a somewhat run-down Manor for the non-stop run to Wolverhampton.

It was indeed significant of the general usefulness of the Dukedogs in the declining years of steam that some of them lasted long after the Bulldogs had all been withdrawn. While this is anticipating the next chapter to some extent, I may add a note about the last of them all, No 9017, now preserved and working on the Bluebell Line. This locomotive has the frames from No 3425, always unnamed, and originally built as No 3715 in June 1906. It was one of the earliest Bulldogs to be superheated,

Up stopping train from Aberystwyth entering Talerddig station, with No 9004. *(E. D. Bruton)*

having been so equipped in May 1910. Today, if one reckons the age of a locomotive by the age of its frames, this survivor of the Dukedogs is 72 years old and still in service.

This chapter has ranged over a considerable period in Great Western locomotive history, and there is one further class, in addition to the Duke and Dukedogs that must have its history brought to a conclusion. This is the 3521 class which consisted of two groups, 26 with domed boilers, and rebuilt in that form in 1899-1900, and 14 that in 1900-2 had been rebuilt with domeless parallel boilers of the Camel type. Of the former group all except one, No 3530, eventually acquired flush Belpaire firebox boilers with a dome on the back ring, like those of the Dukes. No 3530 had a similar boiler but the dome was on the front ring. Five locomotives of this group, Nos 3522, 3526, 3527, 3541, in addition to the one with the odd boiler, No 3530, remained non-superheated until the time of their withdrawal. The rest were superheated at various dates between 1915 and 1927. It is of interest to recall that two of them, Nos 3521 and 3546 were sold to the Cambrian Railways in 1921 to replace the two locomotives destroyed in

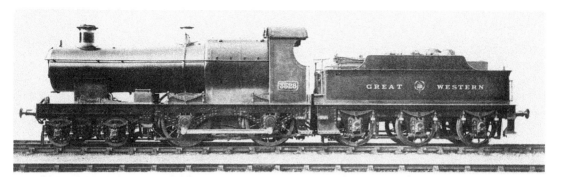

Class 3521 4-4-0 No 3528 fitted with No 2 standard boiler, superheated, and fully lined-out, as from 1912. *(British Railways)*

the Abermule head-on collision. These two were actually allocated the numbers of the locomotives destroyed, namely 82 and 95, but they were not renumbered, and reverted to Great Western ownership in January 1922.

The 14 locomotives of the 3521 class that were provided with parallel domeless boilers in 1900-2 in due course came within the Churchward boiler standardisation programme, and beginning with No 3546 in November 1906 they were fitted with long-coned taper boilers, at first non-superheated. By 1914 they had all been so treated, although by that time the first one had reverted to a parallel boiler, and another had received a short-cone taper boiler. There was no significance about these changes, which occurred in the ordinary course of boiler utilisation at the time of overhaul. No 3558 was the

first to be superheated, this taking place at the time of fitting the long-cone taper boiler in September 1910. Five others were superheated in 1911-3, but it was not until 1923 that any more were so equipped. Then a further five were superheated in 1923-6. By then withdrawal of the class had already started, and three of them, Nos 3532, 3536 and 3556, were never superheated. Of the 3521 class it was the domed boiler variety that lasted longest, presumably because they could be used on the Cambrian section. The last survivors of both groups, Nos 3557 (domed) and 3559 (domeless) which were scrapped in 1934 and 1931 respectively, ended their days at Worcester.

CHAPTER SEVEN

THE LAST YEARS

At the end of World War II there were 53 Bulldogs still in service, 45 of them surviving to come into national ownership on 1 January 1948. During the summer of 1947, the last year of the Great Western Railway, quite a number of them were in the West Country acting as main line pilots. During that traumatic period when the Cornish Riviera Express was suspended, and the 11.00am from Paddington was the principal morning service from London to the West of England, I rode down to Plymouth on the footplate, and with a gross load of 505 tons our King had to have assistance from Newton Abbot. 4-4-0 No 3446 *Goldfinch* coupled on ahead of us. It was a great sight to see the little locomotive blasting its way up the banks, and then leading us down and round the curves, with

In 1947: No 3445 *Flamingo* at Penzance, ready to double-head the up 'Limited' to Plymouth. *(O. S. Nock)*

its outside cranks flailing. The fifteen locomotives of the bird series were the last to remain in service and another of them, No 3445 *Flamingo*, piloted the up 'Limited' throughout from Penzance to Plymouth in the late summer of that same year. We had a 14-coach train, and the King that took over at North Road also needed assistance to Newton Abbot, No 3391 *Dominion of Canada* being coupled on ahead.

Reference to the case histories at the end of the book shows that withdrawal of the Bulldogs continued rapidly in 1948, and by the end of that first year of nationalisation another 17 of them had gone. In those years, however, the railway enthusiast societies were taking-up strongly the idea launched so successfully on the LNER in 1938 of running special excursions with historic locomotives. In June 1951, when only Nos 3453 *Seagull* and 3454 *Skylark* remained, the Midland Area of the Stephenson Locomotive Society organised a special trip from

Birmingham (Snow Hill) to Swindon, and back. I was privileged to ride on the footplate during the outward journey, so right at the end of their lives I had some first-hand experience of these splendid locomotives. Being a Sunday there were several checks for track repairs, and the locomotive itself though beautifully turned out, was showing its age, needing to be handled gently. So, even with only five coaches and a gross trailing load of 172 tons we made no speed records. Nevertheless No 3454 *Skylark* was very pleasant to ride, steaming freely, and working in 25 or 27 per cent cut-off with the main valve of the regulator just open its action was very smooth.

The opening run from Birmingham to Leamington was much delayed, and we had just reached 60mph down Hatton bank when signals checked us through Warwick. The next stage to Oxford was booked in 66 minutes for 42.5 miles, and this we more than kept despite a relaying slack to 5mph in the middle of the Fosse Road bank, and a dead stand for signals at Aynho. The recovery from the first of these, on the 1 in 187 gradient was excellent, to 38mph, but things were taken easily down through Banbury, not exceeding 54mph. The gentle descent from Aynho to Oxford was run with a maximum speed of 58mph and the 42.5 miles from Leamington completed in 63 minutes, or about 57 minutes net. From Didcot to Swindon, working in 25 per cent cut-off with the first valve

SLS Special Birmingham to Swindon, near Uffington, hauled by No 3454 *Skylark* with the author on the footplate. *(M. W. Earley)*

of the regulator, speed ranged between 49mph and 52mph. From some of my friends who returned to Birmingham with the train I gathered that having taken the measure of the locomotive the driver was rather more venture-some than on the outward journey, and attained speeds up to 65mph. The two surviving locomotives of the class, usually languishing in the shed at Reading, were withdrawn later that same year.

In the meantime, what of the other distinguished survivor, *City of Truro*? During the war, when the location of the old Railway Museum at York was too close to legitimate military targets to be comfortable the locomotive was taken away and, covered in tarpaulins, was hidden in the tiny shed at Sprouston, on the Border Union line between Berwick and St Boswells. There it lay completely away from public gaze until the time approached for the re-opening of the museum, still under LNER management, in 1947. It seemed as if the famous locomotive was to remain a museum piece, but in 1953 to assist in the celebration of the centenary of Doncaster works, the two Great Northern Atlantics were taken out of York Museum, and put into running order. Taking their cue from this notable precedent, a

The refugee extracted: *City of Truro* drawn out of Sprouston shed for examination. *(M. Halbert)*

movement was launched by certain Great Western enthusiasts to have *City of Truro* back into traffic for the 50th anniversary of its great run on the Ocean Mail in May 1904. Unfortunately the idea was born a little too late for any celebration in 1954, but with that tremendous enthusiast the late R. F. Hanks in the Chair at Paddington, things began to happen, and in the early spring of 1957 *City of Truro* arrived back at Swindon. It was then in the condition familiar to visitors to the York Railway Museum, numbered 3717, painted and lined-out in the style of express passenger locomotives at the time of its withdrawal from ordinary traffic in 1931. Then it disappeared into the Works.

Imagine then the delight of all Great Western enthusiasts when a few months later it emerged not only in full running order, but in the gorgeous livery of 1903, carried when it was first outshopped from Swindon. It is true that certain

City of Truro passing through Belford, Northumberland on its return to York. *(M. Halbert)*

highly erudite scholars of locomotive history with long memories averred that certain details of the elaborate lining on those red underframes, and on the boiler bands were not *quite* correct, but these were minutiae. The general effect was magnificent. Moreover it was soon evident that the locomotive, now carrying the original number 3440, was to be no mere mobile museum piece. It had to earn its keep, and with no kid-gloves handling either. I shall never forget that Sunday in May 1957, when it was set to work a seaside excursion from Swindon, Bath and Bristol to Torquay and Kingswear, when once again I was privileged to have a footplate pass. The train was well patronised, and we had a load of eight coaches, 264 tons tare, and fully 285 tons full. If one looks back to the first volume of this work, and studies the runs made by Atbaras and Cities in their prime it will be realised that a gross trailing load of 285 tons would have been considered quite heavy, and above daily standards of requirement. On the outward journey a stop was made at Taunton, but returning in the evening we made a non-stop run from Teignmouth to Bristol.

City of Truro, numbered 3717, on its return from York, at Swindon, before rehabilitation. *(K. H. Leech)*

Because of track renewals, and consequent single-line working, we had a somewhat delayed start out of Bristol, and it took 18¾ minutes to pass Flax Bourton, six miles, slowing there to 10mph to cross from the up to the down line. From there we ran well, covering the 28.8 miles to the Taunton stop in 31 minutes 53 seconds. There was a strong cross-wind that hampered us at first, and after touching 60mph down the bank past Nailsea speed fell away to 57mph past Worle Junction, even though the locomotive was working in 27 per cent cut-off with the regulator ¾-full open. But after the direction of the line changed, between Worle and Uphill, we made much better time and the 20.1 miles from Uphill Junction to Cogload Junction were covered in 19 minutes 12 seconds, with a maximum speed of 66mph. Out of Taunton *City of Truro* was naturally not driven with the same vigour as was *City of Bristol* on the dynamometer car test run of July 1903, but we certainly did extremely well. The locomotive was worked in 33 to 37 per cent cut-off with a full open regulator. We touched 48mph through Wellington, and entered Whiteball Tunnel at 32mph, through which there was a speed restriction to 5mph. Then we ran briskly down to Exeter, at 64mph to 70mph. The locomotive was a joy to ride, and we finished with a pleasant little spin round the coast to Teignmouth.

I had the pleasure of Inspector Andress's company on the footplate, and he was so pleased with the working of the locomotive, and so confident, that he decided really to 'have a go' on the return journey; 'having a go' meant an attempt at a really high maximum speed down Wellington bank. He had the wholehearted backing of the Bristol driver and fireman, Messrs Veale and Jenkins, who had worked the locomotive down from Bristol to Newton Abbot. So after a day of beautiful spring sunshine in the pleasance of Dartmouth, we embarked upon the return journey with the keenest sense of anticipation. Naturally we were thinking of what had happened on 9 May 1904, but there was a vast difference in the circumstances. The Ocean Mail of that day had a load of 148 tons; we had nearly double—285 tons. While there is no difficulty in attaining high speed down a steep gradient with a straight enough alignment one does need distance in which to accelerate to a high maximum, and with such a load as 285 tons we were not likely to breast Whiteball summit at the 52mph of the Ocean Mail. Nevertheless my friends on the footplate were all keyed up to 'have a go'.

The weather conditions were perfect, and after a gentle start round the Devon coast and a slack to 35mph through Exeter, we made a superb climb to Whiteball. As the tabulated details show, the locomotive was not being spared, with the regulator full open most of the way, and cut-offs between 27 and 33 per cent.

City of Truro on Swindon-Kingswear Sunday excursion, leaving Bristol, with the author on the footplate. A maximum of 84mph was attained on the return journey. *(Ivo Peters)*

After topping Whiteball at the fine minimum speed of 38mph the driver went all out for a high maximum, and the working was left unchanged as we started down the bank; the speed had reached 81mph as we approached Wellington. Here cut-off was shortened to 26 per cent and the regulator eased back to one half-open, but we continued to accelerate and reached 84mph at Poole Siding and on a descent of 1 in 174 practically holding this speed on to Bradford Crossing. We had, however, to cross over from main to relief line at Taunton and this meant a

WESTERN REGION — TEIGNMOUTH-BRISTOL   An Excursion in 1957
Load: 8 coaches, 264 tons tare, 285 tons full
Locomotive: 4-4-0 No 3440 *City of Truro*

Distance Miles		Actual min sec	Speeds mph	Regulator opening	Cut-off %	Boiler pressure lb/sq in
0.0	TEIGNMOUTH	0 00	—	—	—	—
2.8	Dawlish	5 05	50	½	33	197
6.5	Starcross	9 18	(slack)			
10.3	Exminster	13 22	62	¾	27	192
15.0	EXETER	18 42	35*	⅞	33	180
18.5	Stoke Canon	23 17	52	⅞	27	190
22.2	Silverton	27 29	56/53	Full	27	183
27.6	Cullompton	33 18	56	Full	27	190
29.9	*Tiverton Junc*	36 00	47 ½/54 ½	Full	27	192
32.9	*Milepost 176*	39 34	50	Full	33	180
34.9	*Whiteball Box*	42 23	38	Full	33	187
38.7	Wellington	46 08	81	½	26	—
40.1	*Poole Siding*	47 09	84	½	26	—
41.35	*Bradford Crossing*	48 03	83	½	26	—
43.8	Norton Fitzwarren	50 05	72	Closed	—	—
—		slack				
45.8	TAUNTON	52 52	25*	Full	26	182
51.6	Durston	59 23	60/57	Full	24	190
57.3	BRIDGWATER	65 08	62	Full	26	177
63.6	Highbridge	71 23	61	Full	26	185
66.4	Brent Knoll	74 08	59	Full	26	187
73.8	*Worle Junc*	81 30	61 ½	Full	26	172
78.6	Yatton	86 15	62	Full	26	182
84.6	Flax Bourton	92 27	50	Full	26	187
88.7	Parson St.	96 55	58	Closed	—	—
90.6	BRISTOL	101 25	—	—	—	—

* Speed restrictions

slack to 25mph; nevertheless we had made the excellent time of 34 minutes 10 seconds from Exeter to Taunton, both places being passed slowly.

After Taunton with a strong cross-wind catching us continuously along this exposed stretch, it needed hard work on the footplate to make an average of 60mph. For a short time after Durston the driver tried 24 per cent cut-off, but the speed fell from 62mph to 56mph and he reverted to 26 per cent with full regulator for the rest of the run. We had a splendidly clear road on this Sunday evening, and eventually stopped at Bristol in 82 minutes 43 seconds from Exeter. In comparison with runs made when the City class locomotives were new, 2¾ minutes could be allowed for the slack at Taunton, which before the Cogload quadrupling was not necessary. The net time thus derived, of 80 minutes, showed an average speed of 56.7mph. I need only add that the locomotive steamed freely the whole time, and its riding was elegantly smooth. By the time we reached Bristol I had quite forgotten I was riding a resuscitated museum piece.

City of Truro ran many special trips that summer, and for a time afterwards. It was based at Didcot, and put in quite a mileage in ordinary revenue-earning service on the Didcot, Newbury & Southampton line. I was rather horrified one night, however, when travelling down on the 9.50pm Penzance sleeper from Paddington to find the locomotive, still in all its glory, acting as station pilot at Didcot and shunting vehicles about the station. Then in 1961 there was a Scottish Industries Exhibition in Glasgow. Through the enterprise of James Ness, General Manager of the Scottish Region of British Railways, locomotives of four of the former Scottish companies were restored to full working order, and painted in the old colours. They were used in pairs to power excursions to Glasgow for the Exhibition. *City of Truro* was sent north to join in this fascinating exercise, featuring in many unusual combinations of power, on a variety of routes. This however was virtually its last bow as a working locomotive. Plans were well advanced for the opening of the Great Western Railway Museum at Swindon, and to this *City of Truro* was destined. When the Museum was opened in June 1962 I was horrified to see that the locomotive had been repainted, not in the style in which it went to York in 1931, nor just a touching-up of its beautiful 1957 array, but in plain green devoid of any lining. Who the unimaginative moron was who authorised this piece of iconoclasm I do not know, but I hope he has since had time to hang his head in shame!

City of Truro, as No 3440, on up stopping train entering Bathampton—a regular running in turn for locomotives newly repaired at Swindon. *(Ivo Peters)*

CASE HISTORIES

ARMSTRONG CLASS

Original number	Later number	Name	Built	Superheated	Re-numbered	Withdrawn
7	4171	Armstrong (a)	3/94	12/11	2/23	9/28
8	4172	Gooch	5/94	11/11	2/23	4/29
14	4170	Charles Saunders	5/94	2/11	5/17	8/28
16	4169	Brunel	6/94	6/13	4/15	7/30

(a) Named Charles Saunders at first

BADMINTON CLASS

Original number	Later number	Name	Built	Std No 4 boiler	Std No 2 boiler	Withdrawn
3292	4100	Badminton	12/97	10/06	5/11	9/29
3293	4101	Barrington	4/98	3/10	7/11	4/30
3294	4102	Blenheim	5/98	2/06	1/12	9/28
3295	4103	Bessborough	5/98	10/06	9/11	4/30
3296	4104	Cambria	5/98	3/06	2/12	6/29
3297	4105	Earl Cawdor#	5/98	10/06	3/11	11/27
3298	4106	Grosvenor	6/98	11/05	3/11	8/29
3299	4107	Alexander Hubbard	6/98	12/05	8/11	2/30
3300	4108	Hotspur	7/98	12/06	11/11	3/30
3301	4109	Monarch	7/98	–	2/11	3/31
3302	4110	Charles Mortimer	7/98	–	3/11	10/28
3303	4111	Marlborough	7/98	3/06	4/11	10/28
3304	4112	Oxford*	9/98	–	2/13	9/29
3305	4113	Samson	9/98	11/05	4/13	5/31
3306	4114	Shelburne	9/98	10/06	5/13	7/27
3307	4115	Shrewsbury*	11/98	12/05	6/12	3/31
3308	4116	Savernake	12/98	1/07	6/12	7/27
3309	4117	Shakespeare	12/98	8/06	4/12	10/27
3310	4118	Waterford◊	1/99	11/03	3/12	7/27
3311	4119	Wynnstay	1/99	9/06	2/13	7/27

Note: All locomotives superheated at the time of receiving standard No 2 boiler except 4113 (12/09), 4115 (10/10), 4116 (8/10), 4119 (12/10) equipped while carrying standard No 4 boiler.
rebuilt with large boiler 7/03; ◊ originally had domeless boiler. * Names removed 1927.

DUKE CLASS

Original number	Later number	Name	Built	Superheated	Withdrawn
3252	3252	Duke of Cornwall	5/95	7/23	8/37
3253	—	Pendennis Castle*	5/95	Rebuilt	11/08
3254	3253	Boscawen	7/95	3/17	1/39
3255	3254#	Cornubia	7/95	2/35	6/50
3256	3255	Excalibur	8/95	8/11	6/36
3257	3256	Guinevere	8/95	9/16	8/39
3258	3257	King Arthur*	8/95	12/96	5/37
3259	3258	The Lizard	9/95	2/12	2/38
3260	3259	Merlin	9/95	—	10/38
3261	3260	Mount Edgcumbe	9/95	6/25	4/38
3262	—	Powderham*	4/96	Rebuilt	10/06
3263	—	Sir Lancelot	4/96	Rebuilt	7/07
3264	—	St. Anthony*	5/96	Rebuilt	12/07
3265	3261	St. Germans*	5/96	4/29	4/37
3266	3262	St. Ives*	5/96	4/29	9/37
3267	3263	St. Michael	6/96	5/31	3/36
3268	—	River Tamar	6/96	Rebuilt	6/07
3269	—	Tintagel*	6/96	Rebuilt	5/07
3270	3264#	Trevithick	6/96	1/44	12/49
3271	3265#	Tre Pol and Pen †	7/96	10/11	12/49
3272	3266	Amyas	8/96	7/30	3/38
3273	—	Armorel	11/96	Rebuilt	2/02
3274	3267	Cornishman	11/96	8/11	10/36
3275	3268	Chough	11/96	2/12	3/39
3276	3269	Dartmoor	12/96	6/25	3/37
3277	3270	Earl of Devon*	1/97	2/34	6/36
3278	3271	Eddystone	1/97	4/39	6/36
3279	—	Exmoor	1/97	Rebuilt	12/07
3280	—	Falmouth*	1/97	Rebuilt	1/09
3281	3272#	Fowey*	1/97	12/11	6/49
3282	—	Maristow	2/97	Rebuilt	7/07
3282	3273 #	Mounts Bay	2/97	9/46	12/49
3284	3274	Newquay*	2/97	12/11	11/36
3285	3275	St. Erth*	2/97	—	5/36
3286	—	St. Just*	2/97	Rebuilt	9/08
3287	3276#	St. Agnes*	3/97	2/20	11/49
3288	3277	Isle of Tresco	3/97	1/12	1/37
3289	3278	Trefusis	3/97	3/29	12/38
3290	3279	Tor Bay	3/97	5/28	10/38
3291	3280	Tregenna*	3/97	1/23	5/39
3312	—	Bulldog	10/98	Rebuilt	3/06
3313	3281	Cotswold	3/99	6/33	2/37
3314	3282	Chepstow Castle*	3/99	4/32	10/37
3315	3283#	Comet	3/99	11/11	12/50
3316	—	Isle of Guernsey	3/99	Rebuilt	2/08
3317	3284#	Isle of Jersey	4/99	9/11	4/51
3318	—	Jupiter	4/99	Rebuilt	2/08
3319	3285	Katerfelto	4/99	1/24	1/37
3320	3286	Meteor	4/99	10/27	4/36
3321	3287#	Mercury	4/99	8/23	7/49
3322	—	Mersey	4/99	Rebuilt	11/07
3323	3288	Mendip	6/99	12/20	3/36
3324	—	Quantock	6/99	Rebuilt	12/08
3325	—	St. Columb*	6/99	Rebuilt	12/08
3326	3289#	St. Austell*	7/99	10/29	7/51
3327	—	Somerset	7/99	Rebuilt	5/08
3328	3290	Severn	7/99	8/27	1/39
3329	3291#	Thames	7/99	6/35	2/49
3330	—	Vulcan	7/99	Rebuilt	12/08
3331	—	Weymouth*	8/99	Rebuilt	7/07

* Names subsequently removed: Nos 3253, 3262, 3314 in 1923; 3258 in 1927; remainder in 1930, save for 3277 removed in 1936.
† No 3265 (formerly 3271) rebuilt with Bulldog frames in January 1930.
# Renumbered in 1946 as 9054, 9064, 9065, 9072, 9073, 9076, 9083, 9084, 9087, 9089, 9091 respectively.

ATBARA CLASS

Original number	Later number	Name	Built	Superheated	Withdrawn
3373	4120	Atbara ^φ	4/00	9/13	9/29
3374	4121	Baden Powell ^φ	4/00	2/12	12/28
3375	4122	Colonel Edgcumbe	4/00	7/11	10/28
3376	4123	Herschell	4/00	5/10	11/28
3377	4124	Kitchener	5/00	14/11	4/30
3378	4125	Khartoum	5/00	9/11	4/27
3379	4126	Kimberley	5/00	7/11	10/27
3380	4127	Ladysmith	5/00	5/11	9/29
3381	4128	Maine	5/00	12/10	7/27
3382	—	Mafeking	5/00	8/10	9/11
3383	4129	Kekewich	7/00	8/12	11/28
3384	4130	Omdurman	7/00	6/12	4/30
3385	4131	Powerful	7/00	5/10	4/29
3386	4132	Pembroke*	8/00	3/11	4/31
3387	4133	Roberts	8/00	7/10	7/27
3388	4134	Sir Redvers	8/00	5/11	10/27
3389	4135	Pretoria	8/00	4/10	11/27
3390	4136	Terrible	8/00	8/12	10/27
3391	4137	Wolseley	9/00	7/10	10/28
3392	4138	White ^φ	9/00	4/10	11/29
3393	4139	Auckland	6/01	2/10	9/28
3394	4140	Adelaide*	6/01	9/10	4/29
3395	4141	Aden	7/01	6/13	2/30
3396	4142	Brisbane	7/01	8/10	10/28
3397	4143	Cape Town	8/01	9/10	4/29
3398	4144	Colombo	8/01	5/10	11/27
3399	4145	Dunedin	8/01	6/12	12/30
3400	—	Durban	8/01	Rebuilt	4/07
3401	—	Gibraltar	8/01	Rebuilt	2/07
3402	—	Halifax	8/01	Rebuilt	12/08
3403	—	Hobart	9/01	Rebuilt	2/09
3404	—	Lyttleton	9/01	Rebuilt	10/07
3405	—	Mauritius	9/01	Rebuilt	9/02
3406	—	Melbourne	9/01	Rebuilt	1/08
3407	—	Malta	9/01	Rebuilt	11/08
3408	—	Ophir#	10/01	Rebuilt	5/07
3409	—	Quebec	10/01	Rebuilt	11/07
3410	4146	Sydney	10/01	8/10	10/27
3411	4147	St. Johns	10/01	5/10	7/27
3412	4148	Singapore	10/01	5/10	5/31

* Name removed in 1930 from **3386**, and in 1910 from **3394**.
\# Renamed *Killarney* in 1907, and retained thereafter.
φ Renamed temporarily for various special workings thus:
   3373 *Maine* in 10/00; *Royal Sovereign* in 2/01.
   3374 *Pretoria* in 10/00; *Britannia* in 3/02; *Kitchener* in 7/02.
   3392 *Powerful* in 10/00.

CITY CLASS

Original number	Later number	Name	Built	Superheated	Withdrawn
3433	3710	City of Bath	3/03	9/11	9/28
3434	3711	City of Birmingham	5/03	11/10	7/30
3435	3712	City of Bristol	5/03	1/12	5/31
3436	3713	City of Chester	5/03	9/10	12/29
3437	3714	City of Gloucester	5/03	2/11	11/29
3438	3715	City of Hereford	5/03	6/11	10/29
3439	3716	City of London	5/03	5/11	4/29
3440	3717	City of Truro	5/03	9/11	3/31
3441	3718	City of Winchester	5/03	6/11	10/27
3442	3719	City of Exeter	5/03	10/11	4/29
		Rebuilt from Atbaras			
3400	3700	Durban	4/07	5/12	11/29
3401	3701	Gibraltar	2/07	6/12	8/28
3402	3702	Halifax	12/08	6/10	4/29
3403	3703	Hobart	2/09	3/11	8/29
3404	3704	Lyttleton	10/07	7/11	9/28
3405	3705	Mauritius	9/02	6/11	9/28
3406	3706	Melbourne	1/08	2/11	6/29
3407	3707	Malta	11/08	10/10	4/29
3408	3708	Killarney*	5/07	11/11	10/29
3409	3709	Quebec	11/07	6/11	9/29

* No 3408 was named Ophir for first four months after being rebuilt from Atbara class.

FLOWER CLASS

Original number	Later number	Name	Built	Superheated	Withdrawn
4101	4149	Auricula	5/08	4/11	9/29
4102	4150	Begonia	5/08	1/11	4/31
4103	4151	Calceolaria	5/08	6/12	11/27
4104	4152	Calendula	5/08	5/11	9/28
4105	4153	Camellia	5/08	7/10	7/27
4106	4154	Campanula	5/08	1/13	5/30
4107	4155	Cineraria	6/08	11/11	11/27
4108	4156	Gardenia	6/08	12/11	4/29
4109	4157	Lobelia	6/08	8/10	10/28
4110	4158	Petunia	6/08	8/10	4/29
4111	4159	Anemone	6/08	7/10	10/29
4112	4160	Carnation	6/08	4/10	7/27
4113	4161	Hyacinth	6/08	10/12	4/29
4114	4162	Marguerite	7/08	5/10	8/29
4115	4163	Marigold	7/08	6/12	4/29
4116	4164	Mignonette	7/08	8/10	10/30
4117	4165	Narcissus	7/08	7/12	7/27
4118	4166	Polyanthus	7/08	9/10	11/27
4119	4167	Primrose	7/08	6/10	7/29
4120	4168	Stephanotis	7/08	10/10	5/30

BULLDOG CLASS

Original number	Later number	Name	Built	Superheated	Withdrawn
3253	3300	Pendennis Castle*	11/08	9/14	1/36
3262	3301	Powderham*	10/06	8/11	4/31
3263	3302	Sir Lancelot	7/07	10/12	7/32
3264	3303	St. Anthony*	12/07	9/13	5/32
3268	3304	River Tamar	6/07	8/10	11/34
3269	3305	Tintagel*	5/07	10/11	9/36
3273	3306	Armorel	2/02	6/12	1/39
3279	3307	Exmoor	12/07	5/11	2/34
3280	3308	Falmouth*	1/09	2/12	8/38
3282	3309	Maristow	7/07	5/14	6/34
3286	3310	St. Just*	9/08	11/15	5/32
3312	3311	Bulldog	3/06	4/11	5/32
3316	3312	Isle of Guernsey #	2/08	8/11	4/31
3318	3313	Jupiter	2/08	8/10	4/46
3322	3314	Mersey	11/07	12/10	11/34
3324	3315	Quantock	12/08	2/12	6/31
3325	3316	St. Columb*	12/08	3/12	4/38
3327	3317	Somerset	5/08	8/10	3/31
3330	3318	Vulcan	12/08	12/11	2/34
3331	3319	Weymouth*	7/07	7/11	5/32
3332	3320	Avalon	11/99	6/10	8/29
3333	3321	Brasenose	11/99	8/11	4/35
3334	3322	Eclipse	11/99	6/12	3/35
3335	3323	Etona	11/99	9/10	8/35
3336	3324	Glastonbury*	12/99	3/13	6/35
3337	3325	Kenilworth*	12/99	8/10	9/35
3338	3326	Laira*	1/00	12/10	11/33
3339	3327	Marco Polo	1/00	7/10	3/36
3340	3328	Marazion*	1/00	11/11	4/34
3341	3329	Mars	1/00	12/11	5/32
3342	3330	Orion	2/00	12/11	8/38
3343	3331	Pegasus	2/00	1/11	2/34
3344	3332	Pluto	2/00	9/13	10/31
3345	3333	Perseus	2/00	11/12	10/32
3346	3334	Tavy	2/00	6/10	4/30
3347	3335	Tregothnan*	2/00	1/11	10/48
3348	3336	Titan	3/00	4/13	1/36
3349	3337	The Wolf	3/00	5/12	5/34
3350	3338	Swift	3/00	6/10	11/33
3351	3339	Sedgemoor	3/00	12/10	4/36
3352	3340	Camel	10/99	8/10	6/34
3353	3341	Blasius	5/00	2/12	11/49
3354	3342	Bonaventura	6/00	7/11	10/38
3355	3343	Camelot	6/00	5/12	3/34
3356	3344	Dartmouth*	6/00	3/11	1/34
3357	3345	Smeaton †	6/00	8/19	1/36
3358	3346	Godolphin	10/00	11/10	1/34
3359	3347	Kingsbridge*	10/00	1/12	8/36
3360	3348	Launceston*	10/00	5/10	11/34
3361	3349	Lyonesse	10/00	1/12	11/34
3362	3350	Newlyn*	11/00	2/12	7/35
3363	3351	One and All	11/00	10/13	3/31
3364	3352	Pendragon	11/00	7/11	11/33
3365	3353	Plymouth* φ	11/00	7/11	12/34
3366	3354	Restormel*	11/00	7/11	11/34
3367	3355	St. Aubyn*	11/00	6/10	1/34
3368	3356	Sir Stafford	11/00	10/10	1/36
3369	3357	Trelawney	11/00	3/12	11/34
3370	3358	Tremayne	12/00	11/11	11/45
3371	3359	Tregeagle	12/00	6/12	9/36
3372	3360	Torquay*	12/00	6/11	'11/34
3413	3361	Edward VII*	12/02	4/11	9/47
3414	3362	Albert Brassey	12/02	5/11	4/37
3415	3363	Alfred Baldwin #	1/03	1/12	10/49
3416	3364	Frank Bibby #	2/03	7/11	6/49
3417	3365	Charles Grey Mott #	2/03	12/11	1/30
3418	3366	Earl of Cork	2/03	1/11	4/48
3419	3367	Evan Llewellyn	2/03	5/13	9/35
3420	3368	Sir Ernest Palmer*	2/03	8/14	3/35
3421	3369	David MacIver #	2/03	9/10	7/36

BULLDOG CLASS

Original number	Later number	Name	Built	Superheated	Withdrawn
3422	3370	Sir John Llewellyn #	3/03	8/10	2/39
3423	3371	Sir Massey Lopes #	3/03	3/12	11/44
3424	3372	Sir N. Kingscote #	3/03	1/12	10/36
3425	3373	Sir William Henry #	5/03	10/10	2/39
3426	3374	Walter Long	5/03	11/12	6/37
3427	3375	Sir Watkin Wynn	5/03	8/10	9/47
3428	3376	River Plym	5/03	11/11	9/48
3429	3377	Penzance *	5/03	4/13	3/51
3430	3378	River Tawe *	5/03	9/10	11/45
3431	3379	River Fal	5/03	10/10	6/48
3432	3380	River Yealm	5/03	11/10	3/38
3443	3381	Birkenhead *	9/03	7/11	11/35
3444	3382	Cardiff *	9/03	8/10	11/49
3445	3383	Ilfracombe *	9/03	12/10	12/49
3446	3384	Swindon *	9/03	4/11	5/36
3447	3385	Newport *	9/03	11/11	11/34
3448	3386	Paddington *	9/03	2/10	11/49
3449	3387	Reading *	10/03	9/10	12/34
3450	3388	Swansea *	10/03	6/12	10/35
3451	3389	Taunton *	10/03	5/11	11/45
3452	3390	Wolverhampton *	10/03	12/10	3/39
3453	3391	Dominion of Canada	1/04	1/11	5/48
3454	3392	New Zealand	1/04	10/12	1/37
3455	3393	Australia	1/04	8/11	11/49
3456	3394	Albany	1/04	6/10	11/34
3457	3395	Tasmania	1/04	12/14	8/48
3458	3396	Natal Colony	1/04	9/10	3/48
3459	3397	Toronto	2/04	6/10	11/34
3460	3398	Montreal	2/04	2/12	9/35
3461	3399	Ottawa	2/04	12/10	10/47
3462	3400	Winnipeg	2/04	11/13	5/49
3463	3401	Vancouver	3/04	11/11	11/49
3464	3402	Jamaica	3/04	12/11	3/37
3465	3403	Trinidad	3/04	6/10	1/37
3466	3404	Barbados	3/04	8/10	9/37
3467	3405	Empire of India	3/04	6/13	4/37
3468	3406	Calcutta	3/04	3/13	1/51
3469	3407	Madras	4/04	8/10	12/49
3470	3408	Bombay	4/04	10/14	4/48
3471	3409	Queensland	4/04	11/11	1/39
3472	3410	Columbia	4/04	12/11	11/36
3701	3411	Stanley Baldwin #	4/06	9/11	10/38
3702	3412	John G. Griffiths	4/06	5/14	3/36
3703	3413	James Mason	4/06	3/10	8/36
3704	3414	A.H. Mills	5/06	5/12	10/38
3705	3415	George A. Wills	5/06	4/12	2/37
3706	3416	John W. Wilson	6/06	11/11	5/36
3707	3417	Francis Mildmay φ	6/06	9/13	4/48
3708	3418	Sir Arthur Yorke	6/06	10/12	8/49
3709	3419		6/06	3/10	8/49
3710	3420		6/06	4/10	9/37
3711	3421		6/06	11/11	4/48
3712	3422	Aberystwyth *	6/06	1/10	3/36
3713	3423		6/06	10/11	1/39
3714	3424		7/06	1/10	5/36
3715	3425		6/06	5/10	2/38
3716	3426		7/06	5/10	12/49
3717	3427		7/06	4/10	4/38
3718	3428		7/06	3/10	10/36
3719	3429		7/06	11/10	9/36
3720	3430	Inchcape	8/06	10/11	12/48
3721	3431		8/06	10/10	12/48
3722	3432		8/06	9/10	12/49
3723	3433		8/06	2/10	4/39
3724	3434	Joseph Shaw	8/06	3/11	7/37
3725	3435		8/06	4/10	11/45
3726	3436		8/06	10/10	12/38
3727	3437		9/06	2/11	3/39
3728	3438		9/06	8/09	10/49
3729	3439	Weston-super-Mare *	9/06	11/11	7/36

BULLDOG CLASS

Original number	Later number	Name	Built	Superheated	Withdrawn
3730	3440		9/06	4/10	6/48
3731	3441	Blackbird	5/09	12/11	2/49
3732	3442	Bullfinch	5/09	10/11	7/48
3733	3443	Chaffinch	5/09	1/11	5/49
3734	3444	Cormorant	5/09	4/11	6/51
3735	3445	Flamingo	5/09	7/11	10/48
3736	3446	goldfinch	11/09	11/12	12/48
3737	3447	Jackdaw	12/09	8/12	4/51
3738	3448	Kingfisher	12/09	2/11	1/49
3739	3449	Nightingale	12/09	11/11	6/51
3740	3450	Peacock	12/09	1/12	12/49
3741	3451	Pelican	1/10	2/14	4/51
3742	3452	Penguin	1/10	6/11	4/48
3743	3453	Seagull	1/10	11/14	11/51
3744	3454	Skylark	1/10	6/11	11/51
3745	3455	Starling	1/10	5/12	6/50

* Names removed, either by request of traffic department or to avoid confusion with those of other locomotives.
\# Altered names: originally were: —
3316 Guernsey
3384 Liverpool
3415 Baldwin
3416 Bibby
3417 C.G. Mott
3420 Ernest Palmer
3421 MacIver
3423 Sir Massey
3424 Sir Nigel
3425 Sir W.H. Wills
φ 3707 later named Lord Mildmay of Flete, when No 3417
3353 later named Pershore Plum
† 3357 originally Exeter: renamed Royal Sovereign temporarily in 1902 and changed to Smeaton in October 1903.
3704/3414 renamed Sir Edward Elgar in August 1932.

COUNTY CLASS — First batch

Original number	Later number	Name	Built	Superheated	Withdrawn
3473	3800	County of Middlesex	5/04	9/11	3/31
3474	3831	County of Berks	6/04	5/10	11/30
3475	3832	County of Wilts	6/04	11/10	5/30
3476	3833	County of Dorset	8/04	2/11	2/30
3477	3834	County of Somerset	8/04	1/12	11/33
3478	3835	County of Devon	8/04	10/09	1/31
3479	3836	County of Warwick	10/04	2/13	11/31
3480	3837	County of Stafford	10/04	7/11	3/31
3481	3838	County of Glamorgan	10/04	2/12	8/30
3482	3839	County of Pembroke	10/04	4/10	3/30

Later batches

Number	Name	Built	Superheated	Withdrawn
3801	County Carlow	10/06	5/12	4/31
3802	County Clare	10/06	4/10	5/31
3803	County Cork	10/06	10/10	1/32
3804	County Dublin	10/06	11/09	3/31
3805	County Kerry*	10/06	8/12	5/33
3806	County Kildare	11/06	9/13	2/31
3807	County Kilkenny	11/06	2/10	12/30
3808	County Limerick	11/06	10/10	10/31
3809	County Wexford	11/06	2/10	9/31
3810	County Wicklow	11/06	7/10	3/31
3811	County of Bucks	11/06	4/12	1/31
3812	County of Cardigan	11/06	5/11	7/32
3813	County of Carmarthen	11/06	4/11	11/31
3814	County of Chester	11/06	2/11	6/33
3815	County of Hants	11/06	7/10	1/32
3816	County of Leicester	12/06	10/10	9/31
3817	County of Monmouth	12/06	10/10	1/31
3818	County of Radnor	12/06	10/10	8/31
3819	County of Salop	12/06	6/12	5/31
3820	County of Worcester	12/06	10/11	5/31
3821	County of Bedford	12/11	When built	9/31
3822	County of Brecon	12/11	When built	4/33
3823	County of Carnarvon	12/11	When built	4/31
3824	County of Cornwall	12/11	When built	3/31
3825	County of Denbigh	12/11	When built	3/31
3826	County of Flint	1/12	When built	8/31
3827	County of Gloucester	1/12	When built	12/31
3828	County of Hereford	1/12	When built	3/33
3829	County of Merioneth	1/12	When built	2/32
3830	County of Oxford	2/12	When built	2/31

* No 3805 had No 2 standard boiler from November 1907 till May 1909.

3521 CLASS   1. With domed (2301 class) boilers

Number	Date rebuilt as 4-4-0	Superheated	Withdrawn
3521	8/99	12/20	10/31
3522	5/99	–	1/25
3523	10/99	6/15	5/27
3526	6/00	–	10/27
3527	2/00	–	4/27
3529	4/00	7/16	4/31
3530	11/99	–	3/22
3534	12/99	4/18	10/27
3535	8/99	6/15	12/28
3537	5/99	8/17	9/28
3538	10/00	8/24	7/27
3539	1/00	5/16	10/27
3541	10/99	–	10/13
3542	3/99	9/17	3/26
3543	9/99	7/15	9/28
3544	5/00	8/15	2/27
3545	8/00	4/16	4/31
3546	1/00	11/15	3/27
3549	8/99	9/21	9/28
3550	7/00	9/17	10/29
3552	10/00	1/20	11/29
3553	1/99	11/21	11/28
3554	2/00	4/27	6/30
3555	4/00	5/18	9/29
3557	11/99	5/25	5/34
3560	9/99	4/20	10/23

3521 CLASS   2. With domeless boilers

Number	Date rebuilt as 4-4-0	Superheated (long-coned boiler)	Withdrawn
3524	3/02	12/23	10/27
3525	3/01	9/13	5/29
3528	6/00	5/12	7/27
3581	6/01	10/11	11/27
3532	10/02	–	3/23
3533	6/01	9/25	2/29
3536	10/01	–	11/26
3540	9/00	11/12	11/27
3547	1/02	9/12	10/27
3548	3/01	1/26	8/29
3551	12/00	6/26	6/29
3556	8/01	–	10/27
3558	12/01	9/10	9/23
3559	1/01	10/23	11/31

3200/9000 CLASS (DUKEDOGS)

Number when built	Frames	Replaced	Built	Withdrawn
3200	3422	3288	5/36	3/55
3201	3412	3263	4/36	4/54
3202	3416	3286	6/36	5/54
3203	3424	3275	7/36	10/55
3204	3439	3271	8/36	6/60
3205	3413	3255	9/36	7/59
3206	3428	3267	11/36	8/48
3207	3410	3274	12/36	7/48
3208	3403	3285	2/37	7/57
3209	3392	3277	2/37	7/57
3210	3402	3269	4/37	7/57
3211	3415	3281	3/37	7/57
3212	3405	3261	5/37	7/57
3213	3374	3257	7/37	12/58
3214	3434	3252	8/37	10/60
3215	3420	3262	10/37	6/60
3216	3404	3282	12/37	7/57
3217	3425	3258	3/38	10/60*
3218	3380	3266	4/38	6/60
3219	3427	3260	6/38	11/48
3220	3414	3279	11/38	7/57
3221	3411	3259	11/38	12/58
3222	3436	3278	12/38	8/57
3223	3423	3253	2/39	7/57
3224	3409	3290	2/39	9/57
3225	3437	3268	4/39	8/57
3226	3390	3270	6/39	8/57
3227	3433	3280	6/39	8/57
3228	3429	3256	11/39	9/57

The locomotives of this class were renumbered in July/September 1946 9000-9028 in the same order. The names that Nos. 3200-3212 briefly bore, and those allocated to Nos. 3213-3219 are given in Chapter 6.

* Preserved; now working on the Bluebell Line, Sussex.

INDEX

Page numbers in italic type indicate illustrations

Printed in the USA
CPSIA information can be obtained
at www.ICGtesting.com
JSHW052019140824
68134JS00027B/2551

9 781446 306475